LARGE-PRINT
GREAT BIG
CROSSWORDS™

KAPPA Books

Visit us at www.kappabooks.com

PUZZLE 1

ACROSS

1 Florida city
6 C&W singer Black
11 Outcast
12 Sweatshirt variety
13 Certain wager
14 Looks forward to
15 Umbrella supports
16 Broadway dud
18 Sets for "ER" and "Grey's Anatomy" (abbr.)
19 1002, to Caesar
20 Formerly did (2 wds.)
22 Unexpected obstacle
24 Book jacket info
25 Grind one's teeth
27 Put in office
30 Less decorated
32 West and others
34 Hershey's Reese's __
36 Mouse's kin
37 Morning drops
38 Bowler and derby
40 Hollywood's Preminger
41 Showered
43 Firearm's force
45 Gives out in shares
46 "The Old Folks __" (2 wds.)
47 Ridges
48 Item in a British bakery

DOWN

1 Parking at LaGuardia
2 "1,001 __ Nights"
3 Karaoke needs
4 Loving caress
5 "Moby-Dick" captain
6 Pasture clanger
7 Mauna __
8 Simpleton
9 Part of TNT
10 Mrs. Dick Tracy
11 Beauty parlor sets, for short
12 Wheel-running rodent
17 Parisian assent
21 Consider
23 __ Lewis on "The Office"
24 Yarns
26 Perfumed pouches
28 Animated motion picture
29 British after-noon ritual
31 Superlative ending
33 Pilfered
34 Dr. Norman Vincent __
35 Song from the Beatles' "White Album" (2 wds.)
37 Make pictures
39 Married women in Madrid (abbr.)
40 Eight, in Madrid
42 Negating word
44 List-ending abbr.

PUZZLE 2

ACROSS

1 "If __ My Way" (Bing Crosby film, 2 wds.)
5 Robins, e.g.
10 Disconnected from Wi-Fi
13 Prepare to be knighted
14 Sunshade
15 Diving gear
16 Donahue or Aikman
17 Inc., to a Brit
19 "Your time __!" (2 wds.)
20 Motor fluid
21 6/6/44 (hyph.)
22 Investigators (abbr.)
23 Join together
25 Identical
27 City on Puget Sound
29 Reagan and Sinatra
33 They run for office (abbr.)
35 Common kid infection
36 Hoof sound
39 Scratch's target
41 Yale student
42 "WKRP" alum Anderson
43 Gentleman
44 Peter of "Columbo"
45 Stadium
47 Read tea leaves, perhaps
49 Obstacles
50 Rental cars
51 Conga line music
52 Heart tests (abbr.)

DOWN

1 "Now __ me down..." (2 wds.)
2 To each __ own
3 Comfortable as __ shoe (2 wds.)
4 Burke and others
5 Library's contents (abbr.)
6 Event
7 Employ again
8 First public appearance
9 Wallops
10 Say "no thanks" (2 wds.)
11 Alternative to oatmeal
12 Romp
18 Actress Cannon
21 Early stage in a home reno
24 Ice cream parlor extras
26 Prepare potatoes
28 Actress MacGraw et al.
30 Become wrinkled
31 "Old __" (Disney dog movie)
32 Large nails
34 Suffocate
36 Caste
37 Luft or Doone
38 Ryan or Tatum
40 Robber
44 Bogs
46 Happy __ clam (2 wds.)
48 Dusting cloth

PUZZLE 3

ACROSS

1 Threatening expression
6 Harvest crops
10 Magi count
11 Stimulate
14 "Who knows what will happen!" (4 wds.)
17 Extremely
18 Family dwelling
19 College deg.
20 Shiny paints
23 Needed a bandage
24 Swampy ground
25 Cost
26 Tour by ship
29 Nursery stock
30 Breathing organs
31 Mark time
32 "You're __ much trouble!" (2 wds.)
33 Winter apple
36 Certain bug
37 Spy Mata __
38 Mop & __
40 Defensive structure
44 Sap
45 Menu
46 Floating ice mass
47 Oklahoma city

DOWN

1 Doctor's word for "quick"
2 Actress Sevigny
3 Leisure suit fabric
4 Spider's weaving
5 Director Spike __
6 Repair shoes
7 Finals
8 Farm measure
9 Pizza __
12 Lily of "Short Cuts"
13 Consequence
15 Yonder
16 Gets hazy
21 Friend (Sp.)
22 Hit-or-__
23 Obnoxious kids
25 Ballet move
26 Rocky ledge
27 Be almost out of (2 wds.)
28 Not positive
29 Sudden fear
31 Electrician's specialty
33 Thin, crisp biscuit
34 "Just __" (No Doubt song, 2 wds.)
35 Schemes
37 Go backpack-ing
39 Draft status (hyph.)
41 Bar bill
42 Play part
43 Greek letter

PUZZLE 4

ACROSS

1 "Full speed __!"
6 Massachusetts city
11 Klum of "Project Runway"
12 PGA pro Lee
15 Creme-filled cookies
16 Alpine singer
17 Miss Piggy's pronoun
18 Holbrook and Linden
20 Risqué
21 Biblical patriarch
23 Exude
25 Air hero
26 City in New Mexico
28 "Horrible" cartoon Viking
30 Dopey or Sneezy
32 Penny pincher
33 Sully
34 Slippery critters
35 Busy mo. at the IRS
36 Comic Caesar et al.
38 Express, for short
42 Lt. Kojak
44 Quartet after E
46 Slangy "yes"
47 Interlace
49 Curbs
51 One who sells houses
52 Palmer of the PGA
53 Some pre-college exams (abbr.)
54 __ Earp

DOWN

1 "Oh give me __..." (2 wds.)
2 Marsh wader
3 String after "had a farm"
4 Confusion
5 Chef's creation
6 One Direction singer Harry
7 Got out of bed
8 Directed
9 Stunt rider Knievel
10 Gas __
13 Jalopy replacer (2 wds.)
14 Edict
19 __ this date (now, 2 wds.)
22 "Spider-Man" creator Lee
24 Collins of Genesis
27 Crafts
29 CEO's aide
30 Novelist du Maurier
31 Surveillance setup
32 Screening
33 __ Tots
34 Lawn finishers
37 "Otherwise..." (2 wds.)
39 "Laughing" predator
40 Enclose payment
41 Unhappy
43 Harry Potter pets
45 "__ Mommy Kissing Santa Claus" (2 wds.)
48 Give __ go (2 wds.)
50 "__ a Little Tenderness"

PUZZLE 5

ACROSS

1 Jessica of "Sin City"
5 Use thread
8 Feature of Letterman's smile
11 Mold
12 Shakespeare's river
14 Olive __ of cartoons
15 Certain appliances
16 Euro's predecessor in Italy
17 Marine carnivore (2 wds.)
19 Melba __
20 Sudden fear
21 TV selection
23 Mascara recipients
25 "__ we forget"
26 "__ Fool to Want You" (2 wds.)
27 Final Four org.
31 Nautical cry
33 Washed-up star (hyph.)
37 Did wrong
38 Bert's buddy on "Sesame Street"
39 Achieves
41 Aldrin's landing spot
42 "__ a Feeling" (2 wds.)
43 Cereal grain
44 Air pollution
45 Simple
46 GI's hangout
47 Letters in a soldier's address
48 Company's CEO (abbr.)

DOWN

1 Morocco's continent
2 Goofy
3 Bank position (2 wds.)
4 Morning times (abbr.)
5 Beauty __
6 Bottled water brand
7 Poorer
8 Church music
9 Sailor's assent (2 wds.)
10 Aircrafts
13 The N of NASA (abbr.)
18 Merry tune
19 Profs' helpers (abbr.)
22 Receive, as news
24 Construction area
27 Author Roberts
28 Len known for "Sweeney Todd"
29 Indoor sports venues
30 Piles on (2 wds.)
31 Observe
32 Davis and Midler
33 Shortens a skirt
34 Cooking output
35 Read a diary, e.g.
36 Church game
40 Rushed
42 Brat

PUZZLE 6

ACROSS
1 Family quarrel
5 "Murder, __"
8 "Again!"
10 Suez et al.
13 Emulate Spielberg
14 Aviator Earhart
15 Suburban or meteor suffix
16 Jr., often
18 56, to Caesar
19 Rugged rock
21 Anderson Cooper and Lester Holt, e.g.
24 Marisa of "My Cousin Vinny"
26 Garden of Eden dweller
27 Ingenuous
29 Prohibited
32 Discharge a debt (2 wds.)
36 Walks to an exit (2 wds.)
37 Adhesive item
38 Tiny insect
39 Peter the Great's title
42 Where to hear "Weekend Edition" (abbr.)
43 Cling
46 Charlie or Dorothy
48 Loud noise
49 Rapid
50 Psychedelic drug (abbr.)
51 Kitchen finish

DOWN
1 Shriek
2 "Annabel Lee" poet
3 Foot part
4 French noggin
5 "Take Me As __" (2 wds.)
6 Ship's course
7 "Why Don't You __" (Macy Gray song, 2 wds.)
8 Public proclamation
9 Part of TNT
10 Profession
11 Make active
12 Canonized person
17 Verbally offends
20 Kelly and Tierney
22 Prepare a present
23 Squash sound
25 Villain in "Othello"
28 More tense
29 Designer Mizrahi
30 Tennis legend Ivan
31 Like cyanide
33 NY baseballer
34 Increased
35 Lawyer Mason
40 Church alcove
41 Very attentive
44 Mammal contains three
45 Fisherman's pole
47 Stop working (abbr.)

PUZZLE 7

ACROSS
1 Heifers
5 West and others
9 Bush of "One Tree Hill"
11 Before beta
13 "Pardon the __"
15 Quantity (abbr.)
16 Office sub
17 Atlanta-based network
18 Trumpeter Al
20 Dislike greatly
23 Orally
25 Laura or Bruce
26 Reigning beauties
28 Molasses candy
32 Bohemian, e.g.
34 Wall painting
35 Coyotes' home
38 Court dividers
39 Scrooge's cry
40 Highest point
42 Japan or Taiwan follower
43 "Star Wars" mentor (2 wds., hyph.)
47 Lou Grant portrayer
48 Fruitlessly (2 wds.)
49 Carry
50 Dick Van __

DOWN
1 Manage
2 Choose
3 Stimulate, as the appetite
4 Begat
5 Driver's guide
6 Model Carol
7 Heroic stories
8 Glowed
9 Comparing phrase
10 Having weapons
12 Actress Sothern
14 Saddened
15 "Pequod" captain
19 Oklahoma city
21 Reason to rent a tux
22 Not to be taken seriously (2 wds.)
24 Sandwich store
27 Clinging wrap
29 Something for nothing
30 Stays at home to dine (2 wds.)
31 Ultimatum word
33 Lawrence of "Mama's Family"
35 __ Blue Ribbon
36 African animal, informally
37 Correct copy
39 Feather scarf
41 Green with __
44 Dampen
45 Form of "to be"
46 Acorn, in time

PUZZLE 8

ACROSS

1 Patty Berg's gp.
5 West Point, for one (abbr.)
9 Withdrew
12 Surplus
13 Praised
14 Greek fable man
15 HBO series
16 Most certain
17 "__ in the Family"
18 "__ Ideas" (2 wds.)
20 Word of assent
21 Russia's Trotsky
23 Wayside hotels
25 Writer Ferber
26 Quarry
27 Up above
30 Past
32 Used to be
33 Baseball team's leader (abbr.)
35 Powerful impulse
36 Bite from a terrier
37 Where the Ark "docked"
39 Popular frozen waffles
41 Roadside res-
taurant
42 One from Haifa
44 Discontinued
45 Tastes
46 __ today (now, 2 wds.)
47 Poetic cry

DOWN

1 Laze
2 Army "grunts" (abbr.)
3 Seventh letter
4 Expand
5 Copycat
6 Famed NY baseball
manager (2 wds.)
7 Bobbed up
8 Governmental divisions (abbr.)
9 Entertain royally
10 Cast out
11 "On the Waterfront" star (2 wds.)
12 Use a wok
16 Upholstered seat
18 Significance
19 Moving along
22 Congressional vote
24 Attorney's specialty
28 Baltimore baseballer
29 Cokes' competitors
31 Security __
33 "A __ Homecoming" (2022 film)
34 Wide smiles
38 Shoal
39 Columnist Bombeck
40 Empty spaces
42 "The Lady __ Tramp" (2 wds.)
43 Mineo of "Exodus"

PUZZLE 9

ACROSS

1 Bring about
6 Seeing red
11 Affiliated
13 Certain dress style (hyph.)
14 Baby's formula holder
15 Shine
16 Achy
17 Positive vote
19 Thunder god
21 Racing vehicle (2 wds.)
23 __ dry eye in the house (2 wds.)
24 Fine and dandy (hyph.)
25 Emmy winner Baldwin
26 Appoint
30 Humorous play
32 Martial artist Jackie
33 Dunce
34 Conway et al.
35 Sport shoe
39 Before Oct.
40 Peaks (abbr.)
41 Chopped
43 Shaggy beast of burden
45 Famous Hun
47 Jeans cloth
48 Uplifted
49 Mexican misses (abbr.)
50 Popular Volkswagen model

DOWN

1 Hacks
2 Distant
3 Start for "violet" or "suede"
4 Building plots
5 Slithery swimmer
6 Light beer
7 Unwell
8 "Good Morning, __" (1987 film)
9 Having money problems (3 wds.)
10 Lowered in rank
12 Church officer
18 Shaggy beast
20 Bawdy
22 Merchandise dangler
26 Behaves
27 Actress Brooke
28 Embroidery practice piece
29 Second
30 Julius __
31 "Scent __ Woman" (2 wds.)
33 Ottawa's prov.
35 Imitations
36 TV's Couric
37 Have being
38 Get a new tenant
42 Toddler word
44 Farrow or Hamm
46 __ Mahal

PUZZLE 10

ACROSS

1 __ for apples
4 Fido's sounds
8 Growl
10 Baltimore team
13 Cracker-loving parrot?
14 "Begin the __"
15 Handicrafts website
16 Swindle
17 Duke's st.
18 Big Band __
19 Count calories
20 Gumshoes, informally
21 Belittles
23 Fragment
24 CBS rival
25 T'ai __ (martial art)
26 Brat's response
28 Bash
32 Dermatologist's concern
33 Get better
34 Building annex
35 Wise three-some
36 "Begone!"
37 Moises of baseball
38 Ailment
40 Singer Lawrence
41 Boils with anger
42 Pays to play
43 "Friends" character
44 Sock section

DOWN

1 Martin of "Psycho"
2 De Gaulle alternative
3 Folk song girl Nelly __
4 "__ We All?"
5 Apparatus
6 __ of Youth
7 Delicatessen machine
8 Haste
9 "The Hunchback of __ Dame"
10 Woodwinds
11 Decree
12 Pulpit talks (abbr.)
16 Biden's title (abbr.)
19 Pats gently
22 Gradually begin (2 wds.)
23 Luke's dad on "Modern Family"
25 Light conversation
26 Piano exercise
27 Fisherman
28 Dr. __ (children's writer)
29 Remove
30 "__ Lucy" (2 wds.)
31 Attaches, in a way
32 French pals
33 Firefighters' tools
37 __ time (never, 2 wds.)
39 Sounds of inquiry
40 Fri. follower

ACROSS

1 Sunrise
5 Adam's son
9 Honey
12 Detergent brand
13 Lost, as one's keys
14 Law and __
16 Italian wine town
17 Undivided
18 Bobbin
19 Groom's outfit, for short
21 Stack of trash
22 Club officer
25 Main and

Sesame (abbr.)
26 Paper-and-pencil word game
28 Speed measure (abbr.)
31 Speakeasy door features
35 MacGraw and Baba
37 Q followers
38 Having height
39 Enclosed automobiles
41 "You are __ much trouble!"

(2 wds.)
42 "It __ Be You" (2 wds.)
43 Egotism
46 Raised auditorium platform
47 Swiss, American, and provolone
48 End of a 12/31 song title
49 Lincoln __

DOWN

1 She betrayed Samson
2 __ loss (2 wds.)
3 Nintendo console

4 Edward's nickname
5 "This suitcase weighs __!" (2 wds.)
6 Beginning
7 Whirlpools
8 Ogle (2 wds.)
9 Stylish
10 More sagacious
11 Lauder of cosmetics
15 Not Dems. or Inds.
17 Free from duty
19 Pitch adjusters
20 Sudden desires
23 Tree's fluid
24 Fan's cry
27 Observes
28 Allergic reaction, sometimes
29 Entreats
30 Noon
32 Turnpike divisions
33 Borden cow
34 Narrow openings
36 Subbed (2 wds.)
40 Pry into
43 250, to Caesar
44 Exclamation of surprise
45 Opposite of pos.

PUZZLE 12

ACROSS

1 Things to wear
5 Symbol
11 Sioux dwelling
12 Venus's sister
13 In the cooler (2 wds.)
14 Moldable
16 Underground workplace
17 Abbr. on a bank state-ment
18 Neighbor of Wyo.
19 Starts
21 Temper
24 Mamie __ Doren
25 Author A.A.
26 Receive will-ingly
29 Gentle touch
30 Moto por-trayer Peter
31 Cries of delight
32 Milano of "Who's the Boss?"
34 Sound of rain-drops
38 Monogram of Dr. Jekyll's creator
39 Cloisters resident
41 1916 Lopez song
42 Systems
45 Sly
46 Show biz sisters from Hungary
47 Some desktops
48 Romeo, for example
49 Valet parker's wear

DOWN

1 Aladdin's helper
2 Mimicking
3 Some NFL players
4 The __ Gees
5 Cable option
6 Dissolves
7 Olga creation
8 Quebec article
9 Give a name to
10 Damsels
11 Pyramid, for a pharaoh
15 Help for walkers
17 Doesn't exist
20 Neck areas
22 Nebraska metropolis
23 Tom, Dick, or Harry (2 wds.)
26 A.M. ringer
27 Place to get a degree
28 Comic Billy
29 __ Crunch (cereal)
33 Pianist Watts
35 Caesar's robes
36 Vote in
37 Milland and Romano
40 Cold War inits.
43 "Watchmen" channel
44 "Alley __"
45 104, to Cicero

PUZZLE 13

ACROSS

1 Proofreading comment
5 Heroism
10 Bauble
12 Sandwich meat
13 ___ as an owl (2 wds.)
14 Coveted
15 Fireplace shelf
16 Acquires knowledge
17 Kellogg's products
19 Hammer part
21 ___ Moines, Iowa
22 El ___
25 Nile's cont.
26 "Tosca," e.g.
28 Musician Rawls
29 Booker T. and the ___
30 Caviar source
31 Sudden pain
32 More soiled
35 Apollo 11 crew member
39 Positive aspect (2 wds.)
42 Apartment house sign (2 wds.)
43 Bombard
44 "Blue ___" (Fats Domino song)
45 Improvises (hyph.)
46 Reel
47 Elected officials (abbr.)

DOWN

1 Home run hitter Sammy
2 Some Lincolns (2 wds.)
3 Proofed prose
4 Stun gun
5 Singer Williams
6 Edison's middle name
7 Beast's hideout
8 Prophecy
9 Exterminates
10 Beaver creation
11 Remove, to an editor
12 Dealer
18 "Doe, ___, a female..." (2 wds.)
19 Showy actor
20 D-H connectors
22 Zyrtec competitor
23 Charged atom
24 Made a hole
26 Certain number
27 Sharp
31 Mortar's companion
33 Big wind instrument
34 Apple tablets
35 Bank machines (abbr.)
36 Belt holder
37 First Bond film (2 wds.)
38 Overhaul
40 Coming out gals
41 Speech pauses

PUZZLE 14

ACROSS

1 Worked on the farm
5 Corporate bigwig (abbr.)
8 Something forbidden
9 Certain exercise
12 Calm
13 Welcome airport monitor notation (2 wds.)
14 Rogues
15 Located
17 Curved
19 Frolic merrily
20 Cow's comment
21 Comedian Crosby
23 "Viva ___ Vegas"
26 Grand entrance
28 Brokers
31 "Who cares?"
32 Huge hit for the Village People
34 Rap's "Dr."
35 Jane Austen work
37 Actor Dennehy
39 "On the good ship ___..."
43 Like a desert
44 They go to reunions
45 Monastery heads
47 Toronto's country
48 Aches and ___
49 String after D
50 Increases

DOWN

1 Dedicated (hyph.)
2 Fat
3 A mighty long time
4 Accomplishes
5 Voucher
6 Seethe
7 Page for viewpoints (hyph.)
8 New York's Russian ___
9 Maryland-Virginia boundary river
10 "E pluribus ___"
11 Raw material
12 Rogue
16 Like some as-is garments (abbr.)
18 "CSI" evidence
22 Capital of Washington
24 Firedogs
25 Isthmuses
27 "___ & Louise"
29 Talk constantly
30 Mails
33 ___ jacket ('60s style)
36 "Georgia on My ___"
38 Zealous
39 Shoestring
40 "Frozen" snowman
41 Human bellows
42 Mama's partner
46 Ill-behaved

PUZZLE 15

ACROSS

1 "King of Hollywood" Clark
6 Crevice
11 Yard goods
12 Edmonton athlete
13 Accusation against the ref (2 wds.)
14 "Play __ for Me" (Clint Eastwood film)
15 Online exclamation
16 Rights group (abbr.)
18 Perform in a play
19 Claim against property
21 Jet-setter's farewell
22 Starz rival, for short
23 "Surrey with the Fringe __" (2 wds.)
25 Grate
27 Writing assignment
29 Sedaka and Diamond
32 Makes haste
34 Range
36 Busy bee at tax time (abbr.)
39 Treaty org.
41 Glance at
42 Broadway producer Prince
43 Hollow sounds
45 Tycoon Onassis
46 Cartoon from Japan
48 Embraced
50 Frenzy
51 Gives a facelift to
52 Tiny pests
53 Captures

DOWN

1 Technological toys
2 Alphabet start
3 Grain coating
4 Lavender shrub
5 Filled pastry
6 Creates, as a song
7 52, to Caesar
8 "Frozen" queen et al.
9 Go and get
10 "__ Remember" (2 wds.)
11 Feast or __
13 String tie
17 "Misery" star James
20 Between-meals snack
24 Manet and Monet
26 Photos, briefly
28 Okey-doke
30 Situates
31 Shows mercy
33 "__ Little" (E.B. White book)
35 Author Bagnold
36 Separate the wheat from the __
37 Jury
38 Breathing
40 More weird
44 Fountain order
47 "Tell __ story" (2 wds.)
49 "__ Goes the Weasel"

PUZZLE 16

ACROSS

1 Grates
6 "__ boy!"
10 Cold-sufferer's quaff (2 wds.)
11 Beau and Jeff's dad
12 Entrusts
13 Marry clandestinely
14 Gardner of "The Killers"
15 Fix a neglected house
17 Box cover
18 Apartment expense
20 Nintendo competitor
21 Presidential monogram
22 Reynolds Wrap maker
24 Dispatched
26 Assemble (2 wds.)
28 House entrances
31 Elevator name
33 Supermodel Campbell
35 "__, Pray, Love"
38 Individual
40 Covered gray
41 Feline zodiac sign
42 "Morning Joe" network
44 Brewer's product
45 Add to the batter (2 wds.)
47 Most powerful primate
49 Loams
50 Passes a law
51 Nip and __
52 Loser to Truman

DOWN

1 February 14 theme
2 24-hour teller (abbr.)
3 Recipe verb
4 Buttigieg and Sampras
5 What beauty contestants wear
6 Everybody
7 Molar
8 Editors' banes
9 Deft
10 Shacks
11 Neighbor of Israel
12 Actress Irene
16 Had a birthday
19 Pet who traveled to Oz
23 Falls
25 Froglike animal
27 Needles' partners
29 Those of the highest nobility
30 Aromas
32 Scorched
34 Notion
35 "Nightmare" address (2 wds., abbr.)
36 Vowel string
37 __ waste
39 Steak cut (hyph.)
43 Gullet
46 Kind
48 Arctic sight

PUZZLE 17

ACROSS

1 Fish market purchase
5 Leg part
10 Tortoise's competitor
11 Hereditary title
14 "She Believes __" (Kenny Rogers hit, 2 wds.)
15 Supervises
17 Cheese from Holland
18 10-cent coin
19 Knock lightly
20 Cariou of "Blue Bloods"
21 Obedience school command
22 __ monster
23 553, to Nero
25 Without offense
27 Special treatment, for short
29 Recent (prefix)
30 Guest at the Last Supper
34 "Look, up in the sky, it's __..." (2 wds.)
38 Actress Rowlands
39 Tombstone lawman
41 Light bulb inventor's monogram
42 Raised railroads
43 London farewell (2 wds.)
44 Difficult situations
45 Make haste (3 wds.)
47 Jai __
48 Scholar
49 Offers
50 Food fish
51 "Beat it!"

DOWN

1 Knight's tool
2 "Water Music" composer
3 Gucci rival
4 Believe
5 Living quarters
6 Armadas
7 Moscow citadel
8 Folk wisdom
9 Naval rank (abbr.)
12 Creepy
13 Small river ducks
16 Mineral springs
21 Sword handle
22 Dollop
24 "__ boy!" (2 wds.)
26 Low tide
28 Vacuum __
30 Has birthdays
31 Fur traders' stocks
32 Initial stage
33 Having lunch
35 Sloping type
36 Hilton competitor
37 Stop
40 Threadbare
43 Big fuss (hyph.)
44 Punches
46 Young pooch

PUZZLE 18

ACROSS

1 Likewise
6 Finds fault
11 Published diary
12 Seam
13 Andean animal
14 Headrest
15 Pinochle term
16 Lane of "Superman"
18 "Wizard of Oz" aunt et al.
19 __ loss (2 wds.)
20 Franciscans, e.g.
22 Export
24 Swindle scheme
25 Shop
27 Prepare to play golf (2 wds.)
30 Byron and Browning, e.g.
32 Unexciting
34 Nativity scene
36 151, Roman-style
37 "The gloves __ off!"
38 Bingo-like game
40 "Love __ Bob"
41 Three-ring notebook
43 Option
45 Go on a pension
46 Leather worker
47 Dolts
48 Geneva native

DOWN

1 Removes from print
2 Artificial tooth
3 Tailless amphibian
4 Spasm
5 Spoken
6 French cooking
7 Locale of the Braves (abbr.)
8 Measuring device
9 School dances
10 Makes a quilt
11 The __ and the Papas
12 Alcohol
17 Frequently, to a bard
21 Like some wine
23 Dunderpate
24 Indignant exclamation (2 wds.)
26 Homey chairs
28 Spiny sea creatures
29 Castles
31 Countdown starter
33 Nipper
34 Sheds tears
35 Sublets
37 Start of a magical phrase
39 Birth months for some Libras (abbr.)
40 Singer Braxton
42 One of five in Yahtzee
44 "Hee __"

PUZZLE 19

ACROSS

1 Beetle's tormentor
6 Raise
10 Farewell (Sp.)
11 Movie theater passageways
13 Kids' building blocks
14 Lady Gaga, e.g. (2 wds.)
16 Actor Wallach
17 Lamarr of films
18 Ham on __
19 U.S. health program
22 Pedestal part
23 Have-__ (needy ones)
24 Tinkling noise
25 For a short period
28 Casual slacks
29 Tempos
30 Beer topper
31 Young chaps
32 Eating soup rudely
36 Actress Longoria
37 The "Nina," e.g.
38 Family tree branch (abbr.)
39 Person forced to leave his country
41 "Hooray!"
43 Baby tender
44 __ beauty
45 Student's concern
46 Creamery

DOWN

1 Massachusetts city
2 Fred Astaire's sister
3 Stiff
4 Sentimental mush
5 Lisper's challenge
6 __ Janeiro (2 wds.)
7 Catch a glimpse of
8 Capone and Gore
9 Coach again
11 Imitative sorts
12 Turns down (2 wds.)
15 Smells terrible
17 Abhor
20 FDR or JFK (abbr.)
21 Some officers (abbr.)
22 Dirigible
24 Burn partially
25 More competent
26 Makes a basket
27 Went berserk (3 wds.)
28 Brilliant stroke
30 Aviator
32 Bed linen
33 Teheran resident
34 __ a dull moment
35 Renown
37 Army NCOs
40 Plains tribe
41 Bridge action
42 Genetic info carrier (abbr.)

PUZZLE 20

ACROSS

1 Japanese hostess
7 Unwind
11 Cheese dishes
12 Actress Midler
13 Rent payers
14 Longed
15 PC port, often
16 Merry-go-__
18 Terminate
19 Wrinkle
21 Pharmaceutical
22 Myrna of "The Thin Man"
23 Furnaces' necessities
25 Issue from
27 Lopez or Alvarado
29 Is a show-off
32 Least bit
34 Tempted
36 "Diary __ Wimpy Kid" (2 wds.)
39 Pigeon coop
41 Actress Hatcher
42 Last but __ least
43 Impatient
45 Actress Gabor
46 Dutch flower
48 Lasting forever
50 Actor Bates et al.
51 Tidies up
52 Attention-getting sound
53 Mojave or Sahara

DOWN

1 Exits a building (2 wds.)
2 Harmful helper
3 Bouncers' requests (abbr.)
4 Prosecutor
5 King of Judea
6 Give confidence to
7 __ center
8 Actress Barrymore
9 Shorthand pro, for short
10 Lingerie item
11 Lint
12 Reproval from Nanny, perhaps (2 wds.)
17 Indifferent
20 Roman 552
24 Popular movie theater candy (hyph.)
26 Tightly stretched
28 Lay __ thick (2 wds.)
30 Like a neighbor's grass?
31 Footman, for one
33 Look after
35 Radio knobs
36 Like many craft beers (2 wds.)
37 Free throw preceders
38 Map collection
40 __ Lauder
44 Some votes
47 Bankbook entry (abbr.)
49 Numbered hwy.

PUZZLE 21

ACROSS

1 Wager
4 Olympian's award
9 Deep soup bowl
12 Handle (2 wds.)
13 Mertz's pal on "I Love Lucy"
14 Chairs
15 "Ugh!"
16 Farrow et al.
18 Cleanser ingredient
19 Dublin dish
21 Craves water
24 River craft
26 Sow's supper
27 Parts of a play
29 Took it easy
33 Gunfight word
35 __ Tuck
36 Actor Sheen
39 Indian garb
40 Ship's pronoun
41 Jazz singer Fitzgerald
43 Compass pt.
44 Margarita fruits
47 Desecrated
49 "Any Time __"
(Beatles, 2 wds.)
50 Shirker
51 Hanky-__
52 __ v. Wade

DOWN

1 __ State (Ohio)
2 Victorian __
3 Semester
4 Editors review them (abbr.)
5 Shoe width
6 Dispensed, as cards
7 Lawyers (abbr.)
8 Come in last
9 Oval mint (2 wds.)
10 Work on a magazine
11 Webster and Wyle
13 Dares
17 Window frame
20 Comedian Sykes
22 "Fiddler on the __"
23 Mast supports
25 Deborah of "An Affair to Remember"
28 Boutique event
30 One's engaged girl-friend
31 Salaried worker
32 Like prunes or raisins
34 Writer Oscar __
36 Rivera of "West Side Story"
37 Macho guy (hyph.)
38 Height (abbr.)
40 Strike smartly
42 Distant
45 Yellowstone animal
46 Artful
48 Stir

PUZZLE 22

ACROSS

1 Create raised lettering
7 Pinafore feature
11 Agatha Christie detective's last name
12 Artifices
14 Recorded again
15 Beautify
16 Crafts' partners
17 Baby's game
19 Exclamation of triumph
20 Humble reply to a compliment (2 wds.)
21 Compass dir.
22 Wood planks
24 Nintendo competitor
27 Because of (2 wds.)
29 Up to this point (2 wds.)
32 Actor Sheehan
34 Daisy Mae's hubby
36 Lamb's bleat
39 Trouble the waters
41 New Deal org.
42 Tax official
45 "Excuse me!"
46 Pew volume
47 Mariners' aids
49 ___ a dozen (2 wds.)
50 Conclusion
51 Conceits
52 Coloring for maraschino cherries (2 wds.)

DOWN

1 Green gemstone
2 Walter of "The Odd Couple"
3 Some Maidenform products
4 Night to day, e.g. (abbr.)
5 Dozed off
6 Passover feasts
7 Valentine acronym
8 Famous Verdi opera
9 Messy people
10 Submarine sandwiches
13 Winter weather feature
14 Sounds from the bleachers
18 Glances at
20 "Oh, what fun it ___ ride..." (2 wds.)
23 Newsman Koppel
25 Target
26 Spot for milit. planes
28 Not theirs
30 Actor Quinn
31 "___ is a dish best served cold"
33 Certain peanut
35 Los Angeles football team
36 Ali ___
37 "All kidding ___..."
38 ___ as a whale (2 wds.)
40 "Electric Company" alum Cara
43 Popular Muppet
44 Views
45 Corrosive substance
48 Total

PUZZLE 23

ACROSS

1 201, to Cato
4 Hand part
8 Singer Shelton
10 Conceited person
13 Was courageous
14 Makes into lard
16 "__ Tin Tin"
17 Twist to dry
19 Little battery size
20 Mrs., in Marseilles
21 Helper (abbr.)
22 __ were (so to speak, 2 wds.)
23 Trisha Yearwood's hubby
25 Horses' gaits
26 Native of India, often
27 Martin and Jones
28 Track events
29 Shrimp size
30 Fireworks watchers' cries
31 Ivory product
32 Soup variety
35 Mrs. (Sp.)
36 Hackneyed
37 PC key
38 Actress __ Dewhurst
40 Common __
42 Pale yellow, as hair
43 Sources of logs
44 Gomer or Goober
45 Four Monopoly squares (abbr.)

DOWN

1 Demand as one's due
2 Famous NYC venue (2 wds.)
3 Mamie's spouse
4 __ the thought
5 Envoy
6 Like a giraffe's neck
7 Word before day or night
8 Real estate listing abbr.
9 G. Robinson and Norton
11 Home team's fresh start (2 wds.)
12 Distinguishing qualities
15 College placement exams (abbr.)
18 Letters following Q
22 Cairo native
24 Certain colony members
25 Storm
26 Learn about (2 wds.)
27 Consisting of two parts
28 Opposite of fem.
29 Woodward of "Sybil"
31 Construction material
33 Road curves
34 Distinguished airmen
36 Alluring
39 Standing person's lack
41 Misjudge

PUZZLE 24

ACROSS

1 Surprise attack
7 Panama or Suez
12 Smiled brightly
13 Operated an auto
14 Protest, slangily (3 wds.)
16 Breathe quickly
17 506, to Cicero
18 Name's first letter (abbr.)
19 Falco of "Nurse Jackie"
20 Kept in reserve
22 Tear apart
23 O'Grady or O'Donnell
25 Famous New York arena (abbr.)
26 Yielded
27 Bro's sibling
30 North Pole workers
31 Phoenix NBA team
32 Tricky pitch
34 "Tree of Life" actor
35 Boxer Billy __
36 Angling tool
39 Map abbrevia-tions
40 Increase in speed
43 Scoundrel
44 Smoldering coals
45 LeBlanc et al.
46 Thinly popu-lated

DOWN

1 Scrapes
2 Definition
3 Enticed
4 Poor speak-er's interjec-tions
5 Plant beginning
6 Electronics department choice
7 Letters follow-ing B
8 Reach
9 Zero people (2 wds.)
10 Shun
11 Departed
15 Snake's warnings
16 Salon service
21 Give a hand
23 Patriot Paul
24 Wordsworth work
26 155, to Caesar
27 Courters
28 Very strong, as feelings
29 Concordes (abbr.)
30 Hemingway or Borgnine
31 Livelier
32 Winter drink
33 Not edited
35 Unperturbed
37 Metallic rocks
38 Moist
41 "__ Miz"
42 TV schedule abbr.

PUZZLE 25

ACROSS

1 City dwellings (abbr.)
5 Brag
10 "I Got __"
13 Starbucks order
14 Come a __ (fall headlong)
15 Flour source
16 Grade
17 Abates
19 Delta rival, once
20 Colorful card game
21 Garfield's canine friend
22 Holbrook et al.
23 Incite (2 wds.)
25 Bride's mate
27 Fright
29 Duty imposed on imports
32 Land units
34 Capital of Vietnam
35 Talk show cohost Kelly
37 Rights group (abbr.)
39 Bobby of the Bruins
40 "That's gross!"
41 Floating frozen mass
42 Police announcements (abbr.)
43 More like a fox
45 Hair protector in a storm (2 wds.)
47 Toy truck brand
48 Worn down
49 Soaked
50 Baseball team

DOWN

1 Orchestrate
2 Shooting
3 Printed letters
4 It's the "racer's edge"
5 Autos from Munich
6 "__ la la!"
7 Headache medicine
8 Shoulder garment
9 British goodbyes (2 wds.)
11 Follow, as advice
12 Head honcho (2 wds.)
14 Salad dressing bottle
18 Ernie's buddy on "Sesame Street"
21 __ about (approximately, 2 wds.)
22 Bar mitzvah dance
24 Marine predator
26 Pearl Harbor's locale
28 Factual
30 Prohibited
31 Winner's place
33 Composer's creation
35 Corrodes
36 Dome-shaped home
38 TV producer Norman
41 Brawl
42 "Me, myself, __" (2 wds.)
44 Cardiologist's reading (abbr.)
46 Charged atom

PUZZLE 26

ACROSS

1 Has lunch
5 Water mammal
10 What a GPS replaced (2 wds.)
13 First Lady Bush
14 Japanese folding art
15 Jostle
16 Wicked giant
17 UPS delivery, often (abbr.)
19 Load freight
20 Eastern ideal
21 Film critic Pauline
22 Manipulator
23 Undressed
25 Kind of pickle
27 Pilot
29 Emery __
32 Letters between L and Q
34 Shoe designer Jimmy
35 __ the bullet
38 Certain truck
40 Cpl.'s boss
42 Vicinity
43 Departure's opposite (abbr.)
44 Game piece
45 Actress Rigg
47 Blue Devil rival (2 wds.)
49 Org.
50 Amplify
51 That place
52 Lucy's costar, once

DOWN

1 Page margin
2 Med. gp.
3 Florida city
4 Added liquor to
5 Grand __ Opry
6 Actress Bankhead
7 Brass instruments
8 Destroy slowly
9 Less cooked
10 Underground stem
11 Instruments heard on Sunday
12 Freshen, as a musty room (2 wds.)
18 Silver-tongued
21 Eager
24 Bearing
26 Door fastener
28 Actress Downey
30 Pinker
31 Fairway feature (2 wds.)
33 Left
35 Unskilled in (2 wds.)
36 Dubliners, e.g.
37 Torment
39 Whooping __
41 Prefix for gram or port
44 Asian cuisine
46 Good card in blackjack
48 Monogram of Dr. Jekyll's creator

ACROSS

1 Radio choices
5 Moves furtively
11 Use a pistol
12 Late-night host Jimmy
13 Aquatic flower
14 Play start (2 wds.)
15 Neighbor of Mexico (abbr.)
16 Finish for suburban or meteor
17 __ socks
19 Waist cincher
20 Chunk of floating ice
22 Airport monitor abbr.
23 Shade trees
25 Cow part
27 Nods
30 __ of London
31 Pinto and kidney
32 Potter's oven
33 Male child
34 Appear (to be)
36 "Baby Take __" (2 wds.)
40 Sleeve fillers
42 Meadow
43 Mexican snack
44 Make an error (2 wds.)
46 "We __ please" (2 wds.)
47 __ out (reversed)
48 Judges' attire
49 Idolizer
50 Make a sweater

DOWN

1 "Oh give me __..." (2 wds.)
2 Motor lodge
3 Not yet fifteen
4 Everest and Whitney (abbr.)
5 Moves on ice
6 Finer
7 Ambulance worker (abbr.)
8 Run __ (go berserk)
9 President after Eisenhower
10 Rained icily
11 Chunk
16 Some missiles
18 Rabbit features
21 Seashore bird
24 Minus
26 Charity contribution
27 "Dancing Queen" singers
28 The Peach State
29 "Everybody Loves __"
30 Peru's capital
32 Custodian
35 Escape
37 Disney movie deer
38 Group of eight
39 Romances
41 Passable (hyph.)
45 Balsam __
46 Biblical vessel

PUZZLE 28

ACROSS

1 Goldie of "Private Benjamin"
5 Sunshine State city
10 Inconsiderate driver (2 wds.)
13 Drop by unexpectedly (2 wds.)
14 Phrase meaning "plus" (2 wds.)
15 Kind of drum
16 Teacher's group (abbr.)
17 Old Testament prophet
19 Battle reminder
20 Clothes
22 Get one's ducks in __ (2 wds.)
24 Elevation measure (abbr.)
25 Opponents
27 Pointed beard
29 Driving permit
31 Basement problem
33 __ Christian Andersen
36 Actor Neill
37 Cries
39 Small particle
41 What Santa smokes
43 Sicced

lawyers on
45 State official (abbr.)
46 Graven images
48 Import illegally
50 Trip-meter button
51 Flower children
52 Antagonist
53 Actor Connery

DOWN

1 __ at (attempted, 3 wds.)
2 Navy rank (abbr.)
3 "Stop, Dobbin!"
4 Actress Shearer
5 Army figs.
6 Electrified particles
7 Geronimo, for one
8 Desert wanderer's vision
9 Unmoving
10 Make a scene
11 "Just __ Those Things" (2 wds.)
12 Clinton's successor (3 wds.)
18 In a minute
21 Vend
23 Take a bath
26 Comic Caesar et al.
28 __ spirit
30 Business head honchos (abbr.)
31 Winless race-horse
32 Overstay one's welcome
34 Head, slangily
35 Pilfered
36 Steeple top
38 Highway rigs
40 Twilights
42 School that precedes middle school (abbr.)
44 Gullible person
47 Piggery
49 Student's concern (abbr.)

PUZZLE 29

ACROSS

1 Siblings, for short
5 Guns the engine
9 Accept
12 Something worthless
14 Purveyor of secondhand autos (3 wds.)
16 Home of the Cardinals (abbr.)
17 "It's a Sin to Tell __" (2 wds.)
18 Bang shut
19 TV's "__ Is Us"
21 Harmless
23 Wanted poster initials
24 Gossiping busybody
26 Bank offering
28 Scottish dances
30 Supernatural police drama
33 Wheel grooves
35 Express scorn
37 Watch pocket
40 Prime
42 Norwegian capital
43 Anemic's deficiency
45 Some appliances
47 Turf
48 Instant, slangily (3 wds.)
51 Clamorous
52 Ushered in (3 wds.)
53 Visualizes
54 Adam's home

DOWN

1 Slumber spot
2 Costa __
3 Racetracks
4 Continued story
5 Delivery course (abbr.)
6 Historical ages
7 Tycoon's vacation home
8 Utter
9 __ nail
10 Old Testament book
11 Singer __ Dion
13 Columnist Bombeck
15 Clear a windshield
20 After mob or lob
22 Bowls' handles
25 Grad, for short
27 El __ (weather phenomenon)
29 Footballer Bart
31 Blunder (2 wds.)
32 Giants great (2 wds.)
34 Reaping tool
36 Cowboys' show
37 Huckleberry __
38 Nabisco sandwich cookies
39 Kind of knife
41 Appointed
44 Wall St. abbr.
46 Flank
49 Yiddish exclamations
50 "The Flying __"

PUZZLE 30

ACROSS

1 Accelerated (2 wds.)
7 "Dames at ___"
10 Rasping
11 Rock groups
13 Highway access (hyph.)
14 Pressing tools
15 "___ It Be" (Beatles song)
16 Some computers (abbr.)
17 Grunt's counterpart
18 "Take ___ out of crime" (2 wds.)
20 Wallops
21 Ark patriarch
22 Very short putt in golf (2 wds.)
24 Unneeded stuff (2 wds.)
29 Weatherman Al on NBC's "Today"
30 Daredevil Knievel
31 Defects
33 Fixes typos
34 Pimiento holder
35 Pvt.'s superior
37 ___ mode (2 wds.)
38 Friendless fellow
39 ___ Vallarta
41 Verdon and Stefani
42 Debates
43 Actress ___ B. Davis
44 Most like a fox

DOWN

1 Pumps holder
2 Michigan city
3 Corn serving
4 Hang loosely
5 Gomer Pyle's org.
6 ___ up (invigorates)
7 Uppity person
8 Ferber and Purviance
9 Partnership (abbr.)
11 Kingpin
12 Planned
15 Country path
19 Poe classic (2 wds.)
20 Ship's mast
22 Expresses disapproval
23 Honest nickname
25 Grain planters
26 Emulates Earhart
27 "Beat it!" (2 wds.)
28 "Frozen" queen
31 Brought in by plane
32 Tablecloth fabric
33 Mournful poem
34 Gymnast Korbut
35 Accountants' initials
36 Knit one, ___ two
40 Regret bitterly

PUZZLE 31

ACROSS

1 "Bye Bye Birdie" mother
4 Actress Stone et al.
9 Dick Tracy's Trueheart
10 Jumpers
13 "Garfield" character
14 Haughty
16 Soccer great Hamm
17 103, to Cato
18 Have ___ in one's bonnet (2 wds.)
19 Colorful kerchief
21 Actress Barbara ___ Geddes
22 Good cookie for dunking
23 Yellowish hue
25 Snow toys
27 Quick
28 Goads onward
29 Foolishly excited
30 Assoc.
31 Brass instruments
35 Cat's cry
37 Barrett of gossip
38 Chop
39 Unseats tactfully (2 wds.)
41 "It's ___ big misunderstanding!" (2 wds.)
42 Get rid (of)
43 Handle of a sword
44 Used a keyboard
45 Domestic donkey

DOWN

1 Public information suppliers
2 Taiwanese, e.g.
3 Wind dir.
4 Stritch and May
5 Breed of sheep
6 Opera singer Callas
7 Soldier's address letters
8 Sonic the Hedgehog company
9 Pyramid, for a pharaoh
11 Bunny
12 Certain Disney Dwarf
15 Prefix for gram
17 Jacks, e.g.
20 Performer
23 Pre-eruption lava
24 PDQ!
25 Extend
26 "Dracula" star
27 Visited by ghosts
28 A handful
29 Complain
31 Girl Scout's group
32 Immigrants' island
33 Bridge fares
34 Gaiter
36 Bridge seat
40 Snooper
41 Discoverer's cry

PUZZLE 32

ACROSS

1 Radio choices
5 Shoved
11 Courageous
14 Prisoner
15 Actress Plummer
16 Fleeting look
17 Soon-to-be graduate
18 He cured polio
19 __ up (stay silent)
21 Pristine
24 Sp. unmarried woman
27 Method
29 "__ Rita"
30 Hot-tubbing sound
31 Married again
32 Sheeran and Sullivan
33 "__ Got a Secret"
34 Abbr. on a mountain sign
35 June 6, 1944 (hyph.)
36 Speech impediments
38 Mature
40 3M product
42 Soundly defeated
46 "Waltons" mom
48 Exclamation of triumph
49 Eaters
50 Happy-faced person
51 Unit of temperature
52 Otherwise

DOWN

1 Exclamations
2 Image that's a viral sensation
3 Drescher or Lebowitz
4 __ Geller on "Friends"
5 Sty residents
6 Loosened, as sneakers
7 Little
8 Longed for
9 List shortener (abbr.)
10 Report card grade
12 Revered person
13 Chewy confection
20 Grass cutter
22 Famous Verdi opera
23 Rudely inquisitive
24 Jib
25 Sitar-playing Shankar
26 Paul Newman con man movie (2 wds.)
28 Comes up with
31 Inhale and exhale
35 Sweetie-pie
37 Road repairer
39 Purplish fruit
41 Relaxed state
43 Holler
44 Gets by
45 Start playground trouble
46 Quirky
47 Pinocchio's nose extender

PUZZLE 33

ACROSS

1 Sacred beetle
7 Certain GI
10 Detective Queen
11 Biblical poem
13 Police officer, slangily
14 Elected
15 Last-yr. students
16 Boy
17 Pool filler
18 Like a poorly tended garden
20 Actor Elba of "The Wire"
21 "Leave ___ Beaver" (2 wds.)
22 Grows dim
24 Former boxing champ (2 wds.)
29 Shopping meccas
30 Volcanic rock
31 Weatherman Willard
33 Biblical harps
34 Grunt of agreement (hyph.)
35 1051, to Cicero
37 "___ Little Spanish Town" (2 wds.)
38 Social know-how
39 Relieving
41 Write about for a newspaper
42 Main dinner dish
43 Compass pt.
44 Stunning weapons

DOWN

1 Conceal
2 "___ You" (Carpenters hit, 2 wds.)
3 Swiss peak
4 Respond
5 Extent
6 Polar explorer Richard E. ___
7 Singer LaBelle
8 Hightails it
9 Nav. VIP
11 Gun or baking follower
12 Thinly
15 Belt from the jug
19 Wonderland creature
20 Vows exchanged at the altar (2 wds.)
22 Matted wool cloth
23 Labor organization (abbr.)
25 Amass
26 Baseball player from Seattle
27 Gets satisfaction for
28 Space agcy.
31 Scares away a hen
32 Onionlike plant
33 Catalogues
34 Package IDs
35 Make ends ___
36 Actress Turner
40 Vexation

PUZZLE 34

ACROSS

1 Sir's counter-part
6 Musical key (hyph.)
11 Share with others
12 V-shaped cut
13 Fled to wed
14 Battle of Jericho's horn-blower
16 Breaking stories
17 Digital music player
19 South Bend's state (abbr.)
20 Draft agcy.
21 Home of the Aloha Bowl
22 Comedian Foxx
23 Hep
24 Motions
25 Tasty fruit spread (2 wds.)
28 Fable
29 Rustic lodgings
30 On one's guard
31 West et al.
32 Evening hours (abbr.)
35 Model Carol
36 Leaning Tower city
37 Writer Wiesel
38 Des __
40 Call something else
42 Achy spots
43 Not as messy
44 Serpentine
45 Emcees

DOWN

1 Odometer reading
2 Swears
3 Immerses
4 Fruit beverage
5 Act as referee
6 Type of pear
7 Five basic __ groups
8 Some Navy officers (abbr.)
9 Accomplish
10 Lightning's partner
11 Family rooms
15 Tallies
18 Fears
21 Alone
22 Degenerates
23 Grand Ole __
24 Range components (abbr.)
25 Baffled (3 wds.)
26 One's share
27 Pull from the ground
28 Did the crawl
31 Melissa, to some
32 Braid
33 Mimics
34 Fortuneteller
36 Brief look
37 Stops
39 FDR-era org.
41 A-U linkup

PUZZLE 35

ACROSS
1 At a distance
5 "Designing __"
10 Negative contraction
12 "Coming!" (3 wds.)
14 Moved upward
15 Talk given to a curfew-breaker
17 Slangy assent
18 Flat-topped hills
20 Grind __ halt (2 wds.)
21 Grounded jet (abbr.)
22 School dance
23 Horse's pace
24 Scorch
25 Prince Harry's mother
26 Aromatic trees of Lebanon
29 Stock Exchange locale (2 wds., abbr.)
30 Corn Belt city
31 Enter a pool
32 Barristers' wear
33 Western tribe
34 Forelimb
37 Dover's locale (abbr.)
38 Actress Black
39 Antique auto
40 Makes a hole bigger
42 Commended for service
44 Dr. Jekyll's dark side (2 wds.)
45 "__ Ike" (2 wds.)
46 Spacek of "Carrie"
47 Minus

DOWN
1 All in __ work (2 wds.)
2 Forest ranger's concerns
3 Take an orphan
4 Hosp. figures
5 President Woodrow __
6 Very early morning hour (2 wds., abbr.)
7 Apple products
8 Guess at a price (abbr.)
9 Unaligned
11 Battered and fried, at a Japanese restaurant
13 Sings a lullaby
16 "__ Joe's" (2 wds.)
19 Blunders
23 Backsplash piece
24 Words from Scrooge
25 Painter Leonardo __ (2 wds.)
26 Intimidated
27 Famed rapper
28 Stilettos
29 Towel off
31 Jimmy or Tommy
33 Clock pointers
34 "Begin the Beguine" clarinetist Shaw
35 Smokes
36 Styles
38 Singer Alicia
41 21st Greek letter
43 __ will

PUZZLE 36

ACROSS

1 Holmes of "Dawson's Creek"
6 Shake-speare's tragic king
10 Evade cleverly
11 Sibling
13 Chapel area
14 Enable
16 Singer "King" Cole
17 Menial worker
18 Actress Issa __
19 Military wardrobe units
22 Be dejected
23 Feels regret
24 Destined to be
25 Anticipates
28 Meet officials
29 Goes hungry
30 Fizzy beverage
31 "You're __ much trouble!" (2 wds.)
32 Word puzzle variety
36 Letters after R
37 Captain Hook's sidekick
38 Astaire's studio
39 Pied Piper's city
41 Heated gym location
43 Termination
44 Showy neckwear
45 Grounded jets (abbr.)
46 Enjoys Dubble Bubble

DOWN

1 Reeves of "John Wick"
2 Edgar __ Poe
3 __-frutti ice cream
4 Potato state (abbr.)
5 Musket finish
6 Cars that stretch?
7 Sports lover's cable choice
8 From __ Z (2 wds.)
9 Made a second draft
11 Has the earmarks of
12 McCormick's invention
15 Clarinet player's needs
17 Corp. bigwig
20 Crunchy corn chip
21 Ins and __
22 The __ and the Papas
24 Rover's pal
25 "__ Called Wanda" (2 wds.)
26 Classified item (2 wds.)
27 Supposes
28 Shredded
30 Spectacle
32 Wrong
33 Cease-fire
34 "__ a Place" (Petula Clark hit, 2 wds.)
35 Cloakroom sights
37 Long cut
40 Mommy has three
41 Cul-de-__
42 Burnt remains

PUZZLE 37

ACROSS
1 Modern navigation tool (abbr.)
4 More mature
9 Scale start (3 wds.)
12 Walk __ in my shoes (2 wds.)
13 More tranquil
14 Heavenly ones' headwear
15 Problem for TV's Monk (abbr.)
16 "Kon-__"
18 Fitting
19 Suit fabric
21 Popular coffee brand
24 Ferber and others
26 Actress Cameron
27 Arnaz-Ball production co.
29 Squeal (on)
33 Novelist Ayn
35 Diamond and Sedaka
36 Ground for grazing
39 Corporate VIPs
40 Lobster eater's protec-tion
41 Long skirt
43 Apply henna
44 Make __ for oneself (2 wds.)
47 Systems
49 Thespian
50 Hardware fas-teners
51 Wood shacks
52 Deep longing

DOWN
1 Gale and Ruth
2 Season or late beginning
3 Put in the mail
4 Cheering shout
5 "Baby __ Star" (Prince, 2 wds.)
6 Risotto relative
7 Wed secretly
8 Remainder
9 Decipher
10 Chicken chow __
11 Annoyed
13 Planted
17 "__ soup yet?" (2 wds.)
20 Refuges
22 James of "The Godfather"
23 Montezuma, e.g.
25 Wood strip
28 "E pluribus __"
30 Secure with a rope (2 wds.)
31 __ of London
32 Pluralizing letters
34 Perfume weights
36 Ball club's __ hitter
37 Decrease in intensity
38 Company head (abbr.)
40 Lambs' cries
42 "__ to Behave Myself" (Peg Bracken, 2 wds.)
45 Fashionable
46 Pausers' sounds
48 Giggler's sound

PUZZLE 38

ACROSS

1 Civil rights organization (abbr.)
6 Certain soft drink
11 Barks
12 Go by, as time
14 Swivel
15 Isaac's father
17 "__ Hear a Waltz?" (2 wds.)
18 "__ you know!" (2 wds.)
19 X-ray's rel.
20 Remove, as a lightbulb
23 Prohibits
24 Petty criminal
25 Icy rain
26 Wrap around
29 Parboils
30 Beguiling tricks
31 Shark bait
32 Conceits
33 Twain's real name
36 Greek letter
37 African nation
38 Cruet liquid
40 Works toward
42 Blood channel
44 Succession of things
45 Melted
46 Supermarket section
47 Piece of hair

DOWN

1 "__ Blue"
2 Letters sold by Pat Sajak
3 Cartoon chipmunk
4 USN rank
5 Attention-getting sound
6 Chimed
7 Nudge
8 Section
9 Workout spot
10 "Moby-Dick" narrator
13 Worked for a wage
16 Hazes
18 AL MVP in 2007 (hyph.)
21 Loafers, e.g.
22 Army officers (abbr.)
23 Condemn
25 Disgusting film
26 Certain jugs
27 "No More Lonely __"
28 Blown away
29 Throw off
31 In good taste
33 "Rah!" or "Go team!"
34 From Oslo
35 Building plots
37 107, to Nero
39 Youngsters
41 Retirement acct.
42 It follows morning (abbr.)
43 "__ Town"

PUZZLE 39

ACROSS

1 Governments' rules
5 Stalk
9 Made a lap
12 Neutral color
13 A Gardner
14 Playing for pay
15 Amino __
16 Sitting on a perch
18 Greyhounds
19 High spirits
20 Harbor vessel
21 Poker stake
22 Achieves
23 Reading blogs
25 Spanish lady (abbr.)
27 Memphis's state (abbr.)
28 DIY crafts website
31 Victory signal
33 Get together (2 wds.)
35 Charge card name
38 Starting with (2 wds.)
40 Get an A+
41 Blocked out the light
43 Unruly child
44 Midnight's opposite
45 Songstress James
46 Explosive inits.
47 MacGraw and Baba
48 Israeli carrier (2 wds.)
49 Radiator's sound
50 Method (abbr.)
51 Bic products

DOWN

1 "All roads __ Rome" (2 wds.)
2 Report of what happened
3 Move like a worm
4 Lathers
5 Unruffled
6 Speckled __
7 Weds in haste
8 Gym clothes material
9 Ex-veep Agnew
10 Palmer of the PGA
11 Roman garments
17 As of this minute (2 wds.)
21 Green Gables girl
24 With no result (2 wds.)
26 Coral formation
29 Frighten
30 Cancún's peninsula
32 With no trouble
33 Unassuming
34 Flowers' parts
35 Air openings
36 Desktop items
37 Casino machines
39 Highway rigs
42 Sch. fund-raising gps.
43 Car sound

PUZZLE 40

ACROSS

1 Finish a cross-word
6 Seventh heaven
11 Sound from an old chair
12 Otalgia
15 Church's walkway
16 Grinds one's teeth
17 Come in last
18 Actor Tayback
19 Strike
20 Story "guide"
22 Like a conger
23 Capitol Hill figure (abbr.)
24 Hotmail provider (abbr.)
25 Three make a tbsp.
26 Underprivi-leged
28 Western treaty gp.
31 Agent (abbr.)
32 Abbr. on a toothpaste box.
35 "__ it!" (2 wds.)
36 Climbed
38 Mitch Miller's instrument
39 Mop & __
40 Roughly (2 wds.)
41 Tableland
43 More like a fox
44 Religious rebel
45 Show awe
46 Quenched one's thirst
47 Nomads' homes

DOWN

1 Resells for a big profit
2 Camden
Yards athlete
3 Useful experi-ence
4 __ parking
5 Barely get by
6 Reason for a novice's win (2 wds.)
7 Harpoon
8 Money set aside for later years (abbr.)
9 Gets fresh with
10 Lug
13 Cures
14 Catch sight of
18 Gripping tool
21 K followers
25 Kind
27 Art __
28 Blueblood
29 On the train
30 Wobble
32 Talia Shire's role in "Rocky"
33 Sandy waste-land
34 Loves
35 Junior-to-be, for short
36 Another time
37 "Cape Fear" actor Nick
42 Airport abbr.
43 Speedy jet's letters

PUZZLE 41

ACROSS

1 Noah's son
5 Breathes heavily
10 Zodiac sign
12 Use the nose
13 Part of BBC
14 Actress Roberts
15 Rapper __ Kim
16 Korean cars
18 Channel out of Atlanta
19 "Don't have __!" (Bart Simpson quote, 2 wds.)
21 Moon-shaped figure
24 Warning signal
26 Anti-fur org.
27 __ said than done
29 "Oh, man!" (2 wds.)
33 Put to flight
35 Drizzly
36 Welcome information (2 wds.)
40 Sugar unit (abbr.)
41 Dutch __ disease
42 TV's Kelly
44 Sci. course
45 Skilled
48 President Ford and others
50 Inflexible
51 Divan
52 Standees' wants
53 Hair colors

DOWN

1 Popeye and others
2 Crude house
3 Composer Satie
4 Composer's creation
5 Presidential monogram
6 Thurman of "Pulp Fiction"
7 White picket __
8 Swashbuckling actor Errol
9 Bias
10 Julie Nixon Eisenhower's sister
11 Keen-edged
13 Detached
17 Plant beginning
20 Very strange
22 Celebrity
23 Jeweler's measure
25 Vegas light
28 Regretful one
30 Bites like a mouse
31 __ out (reversed)
32 Data entry errors
34 Small branches
36 Transmission parts
37 Four Seasons song, e.g.
38 Last Greek letter
39 Rate of motion
43 Like a Bohemian
46 Cherry's center
47 Football coups (abbr.)
49 Had chow

PUZZLE 42

ACROSS

1 On the peak
5 Opposite of innocence
10 Caressed
13 Asian nation
14 Porky Pig's phrase (3 wds.)
16 Spheres
17 Outbreak
18 "__! A mouse!"
19 Half of XIV
20 Glided
21 Coffee vessels
22 Elude
24 "__ Rhythm" (2 wds.)
26 Antagonist
28 Pass a law
31 Hobble
33 Singing group
35 Small child
38 Parisian eatery
40 Kick __ ruckus (2 wds.)
41 Exalted poem
42 Java's neighbor
43 Opposing
44 Bogey as Spade, with "The" (2 wds.)
47 Pretty good grade (2 wds.)
48 Certain hats
49 Pierces
50 Official stamp

DOWN

1 Certain Mid-easterner
2 Little tykes
3 Gives the nod
4 June birthstone
5 Talent
6 Numero __
7 Layabout
8 Compare
9 Jobs
10 Kitchen need
11 Flourish
12 553, to Nero
15 BPOE's meeting place
20 18-wheeler
21 Bryce Canyon's locale
23 Take out, in editing
25 Fairy tale starter
27 Workout locales (abbr.)
29 Governing body
30 Walk cautiously
32 Turned ashen
34 "Casablanca" star Claude
35 Broadway flops
36 Modify
37 "Ciao __!"
39 Piccolos' cousins
42 "Porgy and __" (opera)
43 Jessica of "Sin City"
45 Bathing vessel
46 "Chances __"

PUZZLE 43

ACROSS

1 Uses the oven
6 Complaining sound
11 Bicycle parts
12 Wire
13 Apollo 11 crew member
14 "Be it __ humble..." (2 wds.)
16 Loafers' bottoms
17 Becomes angry (2 wds.)
18 Actor Wilson
19 Sun. follower
20 "Long, Long __"
21 Doubtful
23 Monastery brother
25 Actress Plummer
28 Soul singer Knight
29 __ module (NASA craft)
30 Russia's Trotsky
31 "Take Me __ Am" (2 wds.)
32 Champagne producer __ Pérignon
33 Miss a step
37 Takes five (2 wds.)
40 Linney of "Ozark"
41 Undergo change
42 Church official
43 Righteous
44 Compares
45 Hidden obstacles
46 Brazen

DOWN

1 "Look out __!"
2 Muddle
3 "Anna __"
4 Yale Bowl hosts
5 ID digits
6 Envy's color
7 Producer's dream review
8 Keats poems
9 __ siren (2 wds.)
10 Posy
11 Old El __ (salsa brand)
15 Smells
17 Tofu bean
19 College deg.
22 White House monogram for 12 years
23 "Alice" role
24 Loots
25 Rousing sound
26 The Louvre, El Prado, et al.
27 "The Morning Show" actress Jennifer
28 Sparkly stone
30 Cut awkwardly
32 Formal combats
34 Guitars' ancestors
35 Novelist's device
36 Norms
38 Actress Reid
39 Men's party
40 Princess played by Carrie Fisher
42 "Treasure Island" monogram

PUZZLE 44

ACROSS

1 Speck
5 Kitchen cleanser
9 Surplus
10 Lilting
14 Pleasanter
15 Approve
16 Tycoon Onassis
17 Grazing land
19 Bullring cheer
20 Tibetan animals
22 Oakley and Potts
24 Slump
25 Product placements
26 Very wide loafer width
27 Title for a judge (abbr.)
29 Corporate leaders (abbr.)
31 Make happen
35 John the Baptist's nemesis
38 Close securely again
39 Naval noncom
40 Written theme
42 Schedule abbr.
43 Canadian province
45 Plumed heron
47 Heckler
48 "__ of Two Cities" (2 wds.)
49 Hunt
50 Rogers et al.

DOWN

1 Shaped like a Slinky
2 Al of "Insomnia"
3 Metallic rock
4 Apartment balcony
5 Hymn's end
6 Tower-building game
7 Plymouth Colony's John __
8 Tic-tac-toe line
9 Fasteners
11 C-3PO, e.g.
12 The British __
13 Average grades
18 Tennis ace Arthur
21 Because of (2 wds.)
23 Grandmas, to some
27 Wife of Zeus
28 Calendar unit (2 wds.)
29 Tapped tree
30 Sphere
32 Double-cross
33 Brands
34 Make jubilant
35 Glance at
36 Actress Oberon
37 Lauder of cosmetics
41 Cutty __
44 McMahon, McBain, etc.
46 Classic "muscle car," for short

PUZZLE 45

ACROSS

1 Canal boat
5 Disheveled
10 Former "Today" co-host
12 Showing a strong resemblance
13 Friend, Russian-style
14 Phone number unit
15 Seafood delicacy
16 Crazy
18 Hospital diagnostic machine (abbr.)
19 ...two peas in __ (2 wds.)
21 Lynx, e.g.
24 Restaurant lists
26 Zhivago's love
27 Bio majors, often
29 Remote (hyph.)
33 Catcher's item
35 Comic Milton __
36 More full of chimney dirt
39 Grandstand part
40 V preceders
41 Brain creation
43 Patton, e.g. (abbr.)
44 Flower feature
47 Small mints (2 wds.)
49 Pianist Watts
50 Punctual (2 wds.)
51 Secluded spots
52 "Yes! Yes!," to a señorita (2 wds.)

DOWN

1 "__ to Watch Over Me"
2 Mutt
3 Vocal
4 "The Merry __"
5 The __ Hatter
6 Hebrew priest
7 Frat letter
8 Kilt's cousin
9 Mythical monster
10 Gary of "High Noon"
11 De Mille or Fielder
13 Restrain
17 Lovable "Frozen" character
20 Disney's flying elephant
22 Dull
23 Insertion mark
25 Ticketholder's due
28 Roman 552
30 Paper-folding craft
31 Lamb covering
32 Flowerless plants
34 Resulted in (2 wds.)
36 Note taker, for short
37 Perform better than
38 Bridle straps
40 Extend over
42 "Hamlet" start (2 wds.)
45 Noah's vessel
46 "__ Miz"
48 Scale notes

PUZZLE 46

ACROSS

1 Twist a top on
6 Growl
11 __ park
12 2014 Ethan Hawke film
14 Talks noisily
15 Manicotti filling
16 It's north of Mex.
17 Roger Rabbit, e.g.
19 Animal's hideout
20 Acrylic's kin
22 Prince William's alma mater
23 Debase
25 Pulver's rank (abbr.)
26 NBC comedy sketch show
27 Sweet age, in old Rome
30 1/60 of a min.
33 Rum from Puerto Rico
37 Door handle
39 Leaning on the horn
41 "__ keep!"
42 MGM star Kelly
43 Gardner of films
44 Armed citizenry
46 Mexican mister
48 Periodic payment
49 Trembling
50 Positive replies
51 Beasts of burden

DOWN

1 Pompous walk
2 Ran after
3 Retitle
4 CPR expert
5 Horse opera
6 Cross the threshold (2 wds.)
7 Manhattan's letters
8 Make __ in one (2 wds.)
9 Pivot
10 Calamine __
12 __ jump
13 Mends socks
18 Toothbrush type (hyph.)
21 Book parts (abbr.)
24 Past prisoner (hyph.)
28 One of the Redgraves
29 Provoke
30 Removes fat
31 Person or thing
32 Lassie, e.g.
34 In the lead
35 Rigg et al.
36 Summon up
38 Radar dots
40 Busey et al.
42 Clear liquors
45 Letter to cross
47 Sounds of inquiry

PUZZLE 47

ACROSS

1 Printing error, informally
5 __ wave
10 Finalize
13 Booby trap
14 Loses il (2 wds.)
15 __ bear
16 Narrow beds
17 __ Moines, Iowa
19 Chirp
20 Gridiron units (abbr.)
21 Load a suitcase
22 Ain't, correctly
23 "I __ Song Go Out of My Heart" (2 wds.)
25 Oven for clay pottery
27 Word after work or moral
29 Cut into cubes
32 Commotions
34 "This is terrible!" (2 wds.)
35 Log float
38 Mower's target
40 Carpenter __
42 Milo's pal
43 Frau's exclamation
44 Surgical memento
45 "My Heart Skips __" (2 wds.)
47 Italian side dish
49 Actress Thomas
50 Passed
51 Manner
52 Certain party members (abbr.)

DOWN

1 Throw
2 "Delicious!"
3 Gucci rival
4 Batting next (2 wds.)
5 Cooking measure (abbr.)
6 If nothing else works (3 wds.)
7 Natives of Copenhagen
8 Eve of "Our Miss Brooks"
9 Jumped
10 Pt. of CIA
11 Scribble on a scrap
12 Social travelers (2 wds.)
18 Sideslip
21 Reimbursed
24 "__, folks!" (2 wds.)
26 Circus animal
28 Soda flavor
30 Passes a law
31 Contribute
33 Holy
35 Rambles
36 Ready to hit (2 wds.)
37 Blazing
39 During
41 Trampled
44 Drenches
46 Ballerina's __ shoes
48 Snead or Spade

PUZZLE 48

ACROSS

1 Asian peninsula
7 Alone
11 Poise
13 "__ Island with You" (2 wds.)
14 Radio wave receiver
15 Fill full
17 Skyrocket
18 Go wrong
20 Opera song
21 Spain's cont.
22 Spotted jungle cat
24 Peter, Francis, etc. (abbr.)
25 Initiate
27 Watch
28 Egg size
29 Fisherman's tool
32 Bakery fixtures
33 __ Beta Kappa
36 Act like Bart Simpson
38 Leia's "Star Wars" hero
39 Malt brews
40 "The Racer's Edge"
42 Opposite of profit

43 Sailboat
45 Most simple
47 Bible twin
48 Good-natured
49 Dweeby type
50 "Iron Lady" star

DOWN

1 Humiliates
2 Wasn't renewed in time (2 wds.)
3 Church tables
4 Max who played Jethro on TV
5 Wayfarer's stop
6 Teen's skin problem
7 Brillo's rival
8 Ready to pour (2 wds.)
9 Dern and Linney
10 Blazing (2 wds.)
12 Beverage beloved by the British (3 wds.)
16 Whiten
19 Govern
23 Single dollars
25 Splotch
26 Roof edges
29 Fargo's locale (2 wds., abbr.)
30 Actress Brennan
31 __ fly
33 "Friends" character
34 Headache
35 Foot area
37 "Picture of Dorian Gray" author Wilde
41 Actress Dawber et al.
42 Truth twister
44 1963 Neal-Newman film
46 Preside

PUZZLE 49

ACROSS
1 Published diary
7 Highest point
11 Right away
12 Comedienne Phyllis
14 Towed
15 Coves
16 Alaskan city
17 Prison weapon
18 Mexican misses (abbr.)
20 Degraded
22 Abandoned
23 October birthstone
24 Thompson of "Back to the Future"
26 Gambler's marker
27 Neck warmer
28 Place with fighter jets (abbr.)
29 Authors' submissions (abbr.)
30 Hubs (abbr.)
31 Uppity person
32 Sore __
34 Chubby
35 Game show tycoon Griffin
36 Texan's tie
37 Right away (2 wds.)
39 Breathing problem
42 Pullman beds
43 Hebrew prophet
44 Previous spouses
45 Choir voices

DOWN
1 Car's pace (abbr.)
2 Elizabethan __
3 South Dakota attraction (2 wds.)
4 Like a checked-out library book (2 wds.)
5 Things
6 Took a cab
7 "__ bright" ("Silent Night," 2 wds.)
8 Halle Berry's birthplace (2 wds.)
9 Converged
10 Sounds from a poor orator
12 Expels from the ABA
13 Equally split (2 wds.)
18 Slender
19 Bird perch
20 Into pieces
21 Car heater setting
23 Musical intervals
25 __ Cadabby of "Sesame Street"
27 Burn slightly
31 Former Turkish ruler
33 Is an Avis customer
34 Sheriff's party
36 Lure
37 Daisy Mae's son
38 John Ritter's dad
40 Deform
41 Contented sounds

PUZZLE 50

ACROSS

1 Hormel's canned concoction
5 Marsh shrubs
11 Pasta topping
12 Winter or summer
13 Receded, as the tide
14 Have relevance
16 Unite metal by heating
17 Long dagger
18 Sgt., e.g.
19 __ Lanka
20 Wrath
21 __ Ono
22 Reproach
24 Do an alarm clock's job
25 Some pre-college exams (abbr.)
26 KP worker
27 Low-down blokes
28 Model Klum
29 English title
30 Fog
31 Underwater craft
34 1105, to Cato
35 Letterhead art
36 Popular Muppet
37 King Tut, e.g.
39 Shows approval
40 Glossy coating
41 Yearns (for)
42 Unwavering
43 Alan of the silver screen

DOWN

1 Cavalryman's sword
2 Government official (2 wds.)
3 Got an "A" on a test
4 Sm., __, lg.
5 Be ambitious
6 Wary
7 Dusky
8 Superlative ending
9 Early U.S. settlement (2 wds.)
10 Rude laugh
11 Stitches
15 Midnight's opposite
17 Failures, informally
20 By __ and starts
21 Mowing area
23 Foyer
24 Remain
25 __ and cream complexion
26 Mexican money
27 Rope fiber
28 To a great degree
30 Lowed, as a cow
32 Officiated on the diamond, slangily
33 Superintendent
35 Tibetan priest
36 Director Kazan
38 Charlotte of "The Facts of Life"
39 Army two-striper (abbr.)

PUZZLE 51

ACROSS

1 Between A and E
4 "Love __ the Ruins"
9 Wined and dined
11 Band instruments
14 Pie fruit
15 Nest location
16 DVR button
17 Scrapbook item, perhaps
19 Caesar's 1,501
20 Richer in content
22 Gardener's tool
24 Evergreens
25 Breyers competitor
26 Inc., in England
27 A.M. show, for short
29 Melancholy cry
32 Tyke's summer activity (2 wds.)
36 Saoirse of "Little Women"
38 __ thinking
39 Supreme being
40 Insurance salesman
42 Friar's title
43 Disentangle
45 Abraham's intended sacrifice
47 Observe closely
48 Argentina's neighbor
49 Adds seasoning
50 60-minute units (abbr.)

DOWN

1 Little shepherdess (2 wds.)
2 Patrol vehicle (2 wds.)
3 Dover's state (abbr.)
4 Some Oscar nominees
5 Cartoonist Walker
6 Sandwich cookies
7 Wind dir.
8 Start to become furious (2 wds.)
9 Prepares leftovers
10 Portray
12 Hot winter beverage
13 Looks secretly
18 Follow orders
21 Oklahoma city
23 Elberta, e.g.
27 "No pain, no ___"
28 Connecticut seaport town
29 Dispute
30 Crazy
31 Previn and Watts
32 Is a boarder at
33 Fling
34 Big paintings done on walls
35 Site
37 Marine
41 Dreidel stakes
44 Lawyers' org.
46 Moviegoer's admonition

PUZZLE 52

ACROSS

1 Scorch
6 Ancient object
11 Poke
12 Lecturer
14 Little Mermaid
15 Cola, e.g. (2 wds.)
17 AFL-__
18 Out of the way
20 __ Jima
21 Boxing bout enders (abbr.)
22 Kid-on-the-swing's cry
23 Corrida shouts
24 Twosome
25 Soap that floats
26 Embellish
28 Small insects
29 Use a pen
30 Complain
31 "Bonanza" son
32 Liquefy
33 Soaking __
36 "__ Believer" (Monkees song, 2 wds.)
37 Biblical peak
38 Postal delivery path (abbr.)
39 Judy of "The Wizard of Oz"
41 Luau greeting
43 Forest's fire-fighting bear
44 Musical notes
45 Snow vehicles
46 Bald __

DOWN

1 Chips, e.g.
2 Unusual knick-knack
3 "Farewell, amigo!"
4 Bigger than med.
5 Diamond State
6 Pinker
7 Wear away
8 Perform dock work
9 Call __ day (2 wds.)
10 Cockpit figure
13 Trireme crew
16 Nosegay
19 Knee-to-ankle bone
23 Egg-shaped
24 Kitchen collection
25 Begin
26 Fragrances
27 Takes away weapons
28 Party
29 Opposite of a Tory
30 Fast food chain
32 Dug for gold
33 Injustice
34 Actress Barrymore
35 Make fun of
37 "For goodness' __!"
40 Texter's "laugh"
42 Mauna __

PUZZLE 53

ACROSS

1 Type of milk
5 Can __
11 Relatives by marriage (hyph.)
14 Timetable word
15 Japanese entertainer
16 Grain of corn
17 Donkey's bray
18 __ glass
19 "Lost" award
21 At attention
24 Pulpit talks (abbr.)
27 Tiny amount
29 The present
30 Neighbor of Md. (2 wds., abbr.)
31 Say without thinking
32 Sot's conviction (abbr.)
33 Give a hand
34 Edison's middle name
35 Simpleton
36 Dirigible
38 Frozen waffle company
40 Scratches
42 Avoids
46 __ nut
48 Argue logically
49 On fire
50 Raise one's voice toward (2 wds.)
51 Dared
52 "Electric" swimmers

DOWN

1 Deep breath
2 Knobby joint
3 Nastase of the court
4 Crushes
5 Acorn products
6 Get the oven ready for baking
7 Typographical __
8 Creator of Mario and Zelda
9 Actress Arden
10 Kin (abbr.)
12 Comic-strip fight sound
13 Place for cutting lumber
20 "__ Got a Friend" (James Taylor song)
22 Monk's wear
23 Ridicule
24 Large mop
25 Very wicked
26 Political extremists
28 Great misfortune
31 Christen
35 "__ Indemnity"
37 Elevator entertainment
39 Joy
41 Husky transport
43 Earnhardt or Evans
44 Footnote abbr. (2 wds.)
45 Gels
46 Cocktail lounge
47 Slugger's goal (abbr.)

PUZZLE 54

ACROSS
1 Bird food
5 Uttered
9 "Finding Nemo" studio
11 Foreign products
14 Leave alone (2 wds.)
15 Joy
16 Clock numeral
17 Dueler's memento
19 "__ Called Horse" (2 wds.)
20 Unit of weight
21 TV emcee
22 Child's pie ingredient?
23 Urge on
25 Shuts loudly
27 On edge
28 Séance message board
29 Light brown
30 Singing group
31 They rank below captains (abbr.)
32 "A" __ apple (2 wds.)
34 Motel units (abbr.)
37 Palindromic exclamation (2 wds.)
39 Buzz Aldrin's gp.
40 Have a meal
41 Beginnings
43 Unleavened bread
45 Actress Marilyn et al.
46 Join
47 Millennials' predecessors (2 wds.)
48 Schoolroom feature

DOWN
1 Bowling dilemma
2 "Old MacDonald" refrain
3 Putting out, as a fire
4 Light touch
5 Wise
6 Download on an iPhone
7 Small amount
8 Female parade leader (2 wds.)
10 Change a Play-Doh creation
11 Nest eggs (abbr.)
12 Severe upset
13 Transmits
18 2003 movie
"Agent __ Banks"
24 "Holy cow!," online
25 Smith or Jones, e.g.
26 52, to Caesar
27 Elly May Clampett's cousin
28 Elevator inventor
29 Blossom
32 Added building
33 Be cheeky
35 Confusing networks
36 Baby bringer?
38 Scary giant
42 Charged atom
44 Pairing word

PUZZLE 55

ACROSS

1 Wharton grads
5 Untidy person
9 Antitoxin
10 Digging tool
12 Uris and Jaworski
13 DiCaprio/ Winslet movie
15 "...or __ just me?" (2 wds.)
16 "It's freezing out!"
17 Jacob's wife
18 Pastrami parlor
19 Fun house shrieks
21 Hoover's org.
22 Marshal Wyatt
24 Food for whales
26 Express disapproval
29 Had an uprising
30 Andes creature
31 In case
32 Police blotter abbr.
33 Dingy
35 Fido's sounds
39 Historical periods
41 __ standstill (2 wds.)
42 Fired clay
43 Sir Walter __
45 Cheesecake art
46 "__ Doodle Dandy"
47 Thesaurus compiler
48 Bad time for Caesar
49 "Dukes of Hazzard" deputy

DOWN

1 Ed of the Reagan administration
2 Cook beneath a flame
3 "Wizard of Oz" relative (2 wds.)
4 Lgs.' opposites (abbr.)
5 Evade, as one's duty
6 Parking place
7 Face shape
8 Advantage
9 Reached base, in a way
10 __ throat
11 Obligated according to law
14 Tot
16 Lahr of "Oz"
20 Snow runners
23 Milit. school
25 Succession
26 Born earlier
27 DVD's sophisticated relative (hyph.)
28 Fronton activity (2 wds.)
29 C&W singer McEntire
31 Wood-turning device
34 Fads
36 Drummer Starr
37 Smokestacks
38 Seven (Fr.)
40 "You __ Me"
44 Eisenhower's nickname
45 Historic start

PUZZLE 56

ACROSS

1 Wanting to scratch
6 Poet Thomas
11 Sevigny of "Boys Don't Cry"
12 Wandered
14 Zodiac ram
15 Stern
17 The opposite of "oui"
18 Cream quantity
19 Liked, to a beatnik
20 Mitt part
23 Skyscraper, e.g. (abbr.)
24 Allows
25 San __, California
26 Crossword heading
29 Prison head
30 Marina sights
31 Loving
32 Picnic visitors
33 Wooded areas
36 Cpl.'s superior
37 Swindle
38 "Be-__-A-Lula"
40 Designate
42 Dwelling place
44 Luxurious pelts
45 __ salami
46 Rice field
47 Pours heavily

DOWN

1 Optimist's phrase (2 wds.)
2 Toss
3 Country singer Patsy
4 Rake's partner
5 Agreement word
6 Saps
7 "__ Sheldon"
8 Hang in there
9 Quantity (abbr.)
10 Annoyed
13 Toil
16 Goad (2 wds.)
18 Holes
21 Stains
22 Elizabeth I's nickname
23 Flamingos, e.g.
25 Citizen of Copenhagen
26 Belittle
27 Cuban line dances
28 Dilapidated place
29 Toil
31 Homespun
33 Discharged a gun
34 Steak cut (hyph.)
35 Gomorrah's sister city
37 Like Yul Brynner
39 Green vegetables
41 Business degree (abbr.)
42 Person who sells insurance (abbr.)
43 Spelling contest

PUZZLE 57

ACROSS
1 Doc for soldiers
6 Bank holdings (abbr.)
11 The Barber of Seville
12 Grown lambs
13 More tense
14 Paleness
16 Art colony near Santa Fe
17 Want
19 Alias letters
20 Domestic donkey
21 Skim over
22 Author Hunter
23 Hike through muck
24 Binding
25 Pretend (2 wds.)
28 Enraged
29 Fruit covering
30 Soon
31 Shade providers
32 Gore and Biden, e.g. (abbr.)
35 Karaoke prop
36 "Mother __" (playground game, 2 wds.)
37 Pretentious
38 Lessens
40 Browns
42 "Brother, can you spare __?" (2 wds.)
43 Singer Caruso
44 Rodeo contestant
45 Vader of "Star Wars"

DOWN
1 Gold-loving monarch
2 Popular frozen waffles
3 Raised auditorium platform
4 Anger
5 Kind of pipe
6 Colorado ski area
7 Lowe or Everett
8 Cartoon frame
9 Mediterranean port (2 wds.)
10 Home to Gonzaga University
11 Crumbly cheese
15 Used the doorbell
18 Enthusiastically
21 Polar transport
22 Observed
23 Peel
24 Sardine containers
25 Hotel room temptation
26 Green shade
27 Confined
28 Tibetan priest
31 Tension reliever
32 Drop by
33 Quilt piece
34 Just okay (hyph.)
36 Image that's a viral sensation
37 Singer Vikki
39 Suggestion
41 Off __ tangent (2 wds.)

PUZZLE 58

ACROSS
1 "Believe It __!" (2 wds.)
6 Scrooge's exclamations
10 Bob Hope's costar Bing
11 Lions' weapons
13 Obvious untruths (2 wds., hyph.)
15 Has birthdays
16 Garden burrower
17 No longer active (abbr.)
18 Heredity letters
19 Talking movie piglet
20 Three make a tbsp.
21 Rigid
23 __ B'rith
25 Mode of operation
27 Group of war vessels
31 Provo's state
33 River embankment
34 Extend over
37 Dog's name
39 Raised railroads
40 One billion years
41 Actress Lollobrigida
42 Aware of
43 Communica-
tion problem (2 wds.)
46 Entertain
47 Guthrie's "__ Restaurant"
48 Killed a dragon
49 Author Anne __

DOWN
1 "Still the One" group
2 Fishermen's gear
3 Bad check inits.
4 President born in Hawaii
5 "The Georgia Peach"
6 String after A
7 "__ That Jazz"
8 Whiskers
9 Clean up crumbs
10 "Public Enemy" actor James
12 Some jets (abbr.)
13 Simpson kid et al.
14 Justice __ Kagan
19 Borscht ingredient
20 __ bomb
22 Dazzle
24 Woody Guthrie's son
26 "Sopranos" organization
28 One who retaliates
29 River mouths
30 Fable writer
32 Imply subtly (2 wds.)
34 Genesis maker
35 Odes
36 Put an end to
38 Oft-printed newspaper
41 Enlarged in size
42 __ in a blue moon
44 Suffix for Vietnam or Taiwan
45 Frying liquid

PUZZLE 59

ACROSS

1 Muffle
4 Bars that are scanned
8 Puppeteer Lewis
10 Storms, as a castle
13 Becomes quiet
14 Cloth for cleaning up
15 "__ You"
16 Paving goo
17 Dollar part
18 Aussie marsupial
19 Sacred song
20 Witches
21 Cuticle scissors
23 Large bean
24 "Much __ About Nothing"
25 Refrigerator crisper
26 Active
28 Go to great __
32 Former Cub Sammy
33 Bull or rooster
34 Cereal tidbit
35 Having foot digits
36 Fitting
37 Raga-playing Shankar
38 Makes beloved
40 Japanese soup
41 Meet again
42 Smelled terrible
43 Fred and Barney, e.g.
44 Canvas count

DOWN

1 Horse's gait
2 Ant group
3 USO audience mems.
4 About-face on the road (hyph.)
5 Touchdown's six, e.g. (abbr.)
6 Contagious
7 Horror movie franchise
8 Derision
9 Asian capital
10 "__ Rib"
11 Jumpy Milne character
12 Preston and Bilko (abbr.)
16 Beginner
19 Actress Lamarr
22 Rose Bowl locale
23 Short note
25 Boxing prize
26 Frontiersman Daniel
27 Depleted (2 wds.)
28 Memory slippage
29 With no opposing votes (3 wds.)
30 Place of safety
31 Reek
32 Finish for lob or mob
33 Markets
37 Grade
39 Suffer
40 Q followers

PUZZLE 60

ACROSS

1 Group of employees
6 One of the planets
12 Extreme fear
13 Stringent
14 Shrimp __
15 Betroth
16 Swiss peak
17 Bypass
19 "Ant-Man" star Paul
21 "Krazy __"
22 Female deer
24 Tile design
29 Centuries
30 __ St. Vincent Millay
31 Washers' partners
34 Stadium shouts
35 Heart test (abbr.)
37 Neighbor of Oahu
39 School fund-raising event (2 wds.)
44 Nero's language (abbr.)
45 Corsage flower
46 Blacksmiths' needs
49 Conduct oneself
50 Flimsily
51 Quicker
52 Mournful poem

DOWN

1 Hidden away
2 Stage device
3 Provide guns
4 Vain one
5 Frolic
6 Comfortable with (2 wds.)
7 Philosopher Descartes
8 Batters' concerns (abbr.)
9 Uncluttered
10 Force along
11 Trickle
12 Peter the Great, e.g.
18 "__ a Camera" (2 wds.)
20 Declare untrue
23 Compass letters
25 Sun. speech
26 Actor Brody
27 Breathing in
28 Nonchalantly
32 Library user
33 Enjoy the slopes
36 Rasp
38 Teeny-tiny
39 Curtsies
40 Good cookie for dunking
41 Spanish eight
42 Genghis __
43 Hand's finger count
47 Oilers' gp.
48 Strive

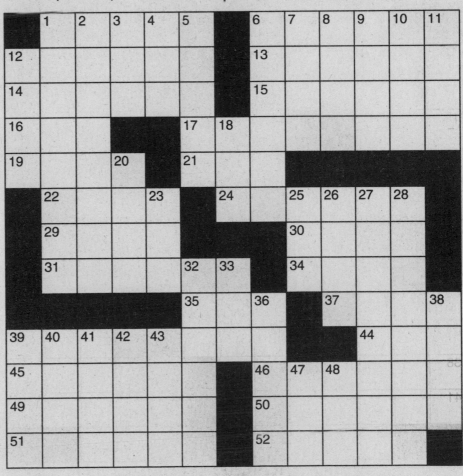

PUZZLE 61

ACROSS

1 Smear
7 Felt sore
12 Symbol of Hanukkah
14 Talent
15 Bric-a-brac holder
16 Evans of "Dynasty"
17 Author Deighton
18 Chew on
20 "__ Around" (2 wds.)
21 Tykes
23 Proofreading note
25 Taxman's agcy.
26 Like a red tomato
28 Type of cereal
30 Part of the head
32 Floating ice masses
34 Skye, e.g.
35 Slangy agreement
36 Elec. measure
38 Loot
41 Married females in Madrid (abbr.)
43 __ shark
45 Falsehoods
47 Be beholden
48 Japanese-style mattress
50 One planet
52 Actress Ryan
53 Laundered
54 Provide funds
55 Some Scandinavians

DOWN

1 Salmon's relative
2 Crater makers
3 Not expected
4 Lassie, e.g.
5 Actor Kinnear
6 Works for
7 __-CIO
8 152, to Caesar
9 Loitering (2 wds.)
10 Pillow down
11 Gentle oaths
13 Warm up
19 "Dragnet" actor Jack
22 Health salons
24 Low playing card
27 Building extensions
29 God of war
31 Ring loudly
33 Algonquin tribe
36 Michael Caine role
37 Lament
39 Prez's military role (abbr.)
40 Ships' bottoms
42 Origins
44 "Don't!" (2 wds.)
46 Erupt
49 Unopened
51 Light bulb inventor's monogram

PUZZLE 62

ACROSS

1 Small barrels
5 Prison weapon
9 Fuming
10 __ wreath (crown)
12 Ishmael's mother
13 Ran out, as a permit
15 Skin care brand
16 From __ Z (2 wds.)
17 Night sky twinkler
18 __ over backward
19 Work start, perhaps
21 Marriage reply (2 wds.)
22 Philly's Ivy League
24 Seth of "Steve Jobs"
26 "__ Street"
29 Tune out
30 Burglary
31 Jester
32 Circle section
33 Slant
35 Birth months for some Libras (abbr.)
39 "I __ Ike"
41 "Rome wasn't built __ day" (2 wds.)
42 Cleveland's state
43 Matt of "Friends"
45 Be stinting
46 Dwell
47 Monica of tennis
48 Hoover and others
49 Extremely dry

DOWN

1 Scoundrel
2 Incite (2 wds.)
3 Parents' dads
4 Mideast land (abbr.)
5 Anglo-__
6 Marcher's syllable
7 Spring bloom
8 Dizzying sensation
9 "Moby-Dick" captain
10 Allow entry (2 wds.)
11 Chief
14 Male bee
16 Actress Bancroft
20 Latin "therefore"
23 CPR experts
25 Witness
26 "__ We Dance?"
27 Stranger
28 Recuperating spot (2 wds.)
29 Cedar Rapids state
31 Field enclosure
34 Types
36 Tex-Mex favorite
37 Clocked a race
38 Soaks (up)
40 Actress Lanchester
44 Objective
45 Medicare minders (abbr.)

PUZZLE 63

ACROSS

1 Blind as __ (2 wds.)
5 Chef Lagasse
11 Ecru
12 Romeo's home
13 Immaculate (5 wds.)
15 __ one's memory
16 Fizzy drink
17 Impress clearly
19 GI's address (abbr.)
20 Farm tools
21 Letters on a marker
22 Daughters' counterparts
23 Jerry Herman musical
24 Remove a lid
27 Wolfish glances
28 Santa sounds (2 wds.)
29 Venomous snakes
31 "SVU" reruns network
32 Touched ground
33 "Eureka!"
36 Trumpeter Al
38 Rani's dress
39 Actress Dolores __ Rio
40 Monthly payment (2 wds.)
43 Infrequently
44 Cooking output
45 White House family in the 1840s
46 Highlands gal

DOWN

1 Fable collector
2 Church game
3 Birthday number
4 Eatery that often sells scones (2 wds.)
5 Avoids
6 Small high plateaus
7 Historical time
8 Lasso material
9 Monogram component
10 Cosmetic brand
11 __ California (Mexican peninsula)
14 Roger or Jessica Rabbit
18 Shades
22 __ Paulo (Brazilian city)
23 British sports cars (abbr.)
24 "No way, Jose!" (hyph.)
25 Most curious
26 __ horse
27 __ illusion
29 Startles
30 Apple assistant
32 New York City's __ Place
33 Spanish farewell
34 Ships' wheels
35 "...__ good night" (2 wds.)
37 Narrate
41 Alphabetic trio
42 Bikini part

PUZZLE 64

ACROSS
1 Sees socially
6 Yearly
12 "__ N.Y." (2 wds.)
13 Hair protector in a storm (2 wds.)
15 Rot
16 Entreat
17 Fall apart
19 Kin of etc. (2 wds.)
20 "__ Gabler"
22 Knight's protection
27 Bring home a pound puppy
31 Orange's category
32 Fatigue cause
33 Utopian
34 Burrowing animal
35 Extra great
38 "Bye-bye!" (2 wds.)
41 Floods of applause
47 Military flight center (2 wds.)
49 Mrs. Bobby Kennedy
50 Not as large
51 Juliet's lover
52 Fast
53 Sluggish

DOWN
1 Word in CD
2 Pet food brand
3 Wrench, e.g.
4 Corrupt
5 Ward of TV's "Sisters"
6 Come up
7 Nominated
8 Small drink
9 Gas pump standard
10 Drop like __ potato (2 wds.)
11 __ Flynn Boyle
14 Address bk. line
18 Professors, e.g. (abbr.)
21 Delany of "Desperate Housewives"
22 Chem. or biol.
23 Camouflaged
24 Suburban or meteor suffix
25 Not permanent, as writing
26 Humdinger
28 "Holy cow!," online
29 Lemon meringue, e.g.
30 Gob
32 Start of a magical phrase
36 Got ready to take a selfie
37 Each one
38 Professors' aides (abbr.)
39 Points (at)
40 Snare
42 Actress Polo
43 "Bring __" (2 wds.)
44 Kin of "alas!" (2 wds.)
45 Not once, poetically
46 Coin hole
48 Pub serving

ACROSS

1 Alice, to the Bradys
5 Exploited
9 Spurious
10 Bellowed
14 "Brother, can you spare __?" (2 wds.)
15 "Star Wars" hero (2 wds.)
16 Star of a coming out party
17 Jetty
19 Famed pirate captain
20 Runway
23 Table sup-porter
24 Wallach et al.
25 More than plump
27 They form corners
30 Woos playfully
31 Contract
32 Nullify
33 __ Ripken, Jr.
34 Royal daughter
38 Upon
40 Move like slime
41 Some com-puters (abbr.)
43 Reading
45 Mantle
47 Plan in advance
48 Great pain
49 The S of GPS (abbr.)
50 Apartment charge

DOWN

1 Tyler Perry title role
2 Excuse
3 Social or journal suffix
4 You may wake from this feeling groggy (2 wds.)
5 Theater atten-dants
6 Puppeteer __ Lewis
7 Long period
8 Day's end
9 Temporary rage
11 Hardworking worker
12 Firstborn
13 Eludes
18 Tell it like __ (2 wds.)
21 Cousins and uncles (abbr.)
22 Cruiser (2 wds.)
26 Wait awhile
27 "Li'l Abner" cartoonist (2 wds.)
28 More orderly
29 Abundant
30 Winkler role, with "The"
32 Spring flower
35 Jungle sounds
36 Utensil for coffee
37 Sparse
39 Baby canines
42 Firmament
44 Verbalize
46 Shirt size (abbr.)

PUZZLE 66

ACROSS

1 Popular condiment
5 Snatches
10 Seafood delicacy
13 Souvenir
14 Another way of saying "Yes, thank you!" (5 wds.)
16 Finishes
17 Amusing person
18 Small number
19 Compass dir.
20 Art __ (1920s style)
21 Corrals
22 Poet James Whitcomb __
24 Trunk's spare
26 Diner
28 Deadens
31 Streetcar
33 Impart knowledge
35 Talk show cohost Kelly
38 Ark builder
40 Golf instructor
41 "Away __ Manger" (2 wds.)
42 Selves
43 Actress Lupino et al.
44 Positive thing (3 wds.)
47 Capital of Vietnam
48 Makes furious
49 Robin's sound
50 Zeus and Apollo

DOWN

1 South Africa's Nelson
2 Elevations (abbr.)
3 __ Kippur
4 In storage (2 wds.)
5 Football field
6 NBA official
7 "Get __!" (2 wds.)
8 46th President
9 Garbage-hauling boats
10 "Doe, __..." (2 wds.)
11 Clyde's partner in crime
12 Pass legislation
15 C-3PO, e.g.
20 One who colors clothing
21 Brazilian soccer great
23 Comics' Kett
25 Gehrig's teammate
27 Kitchen stove
29 Mini-pooches
30 Scratch
32 Mary Tyler __
34 Garden tubes
35 Opposite of left
36 Spouse's kin (hyph.)
37 Patriot Thomas
39 "With __ in My Heart" (2 wds.)
42 Send forth
43 "__ no idea!" (2 wds.)
45 Stooge with bangs
46 To and __

PUZZLE 67

ACROSS

1 Nation's banner
5 Movie star
10 Parchment rolls
13 Glittering
14 Milliner's creation
15 Seoul's locale
16 Target
17 Nehemiah preceder
19 Chessman
20 TV's "Star __"
22 Quartet after D
24 Marx's "__ Kapital"
25 Prissy sort
27 Hepburn or Meadows
29 Industrial bigwig
31 Supervised
33 Actress Miles
36 Distant
37 Touches softly
39 Preserve
41 Reckless
43 Wheel grooves
45 Network launched in 1981
46 Woodwind instruments
48 Apply enamel
again
50 Grand-mothers, to some
51 Mexican festi-vals
52 Personal pref-erence
53 Mark Harmon TV franchise

DOWN

1 Print shop employee
2 Cut off twigs
3 To shelter
4 Coating on pottery
5 Request
6 Popular pork cut
7 Outburst
8 Traffic sign (hyph.)
9 Pitcher Nolan et al.
10 "Vamoose!"
11 Bird's call
12 Seafood res-taurant order (3 wds.)
18 Oaxaca water
21 Novak et al.
23 Couch potato's pur-chase, perhaps (abbr.)
26 Surprised sound
28 Smell
30 Cogwheel
31 "__, black sheep..." (2 wds.)
32 Welles et al.
34 Pays
35 Unit-edHealthcare alternative
36 Forward part
38 Beer holder
40 Soldiers of the lowest rank (abbr.)
42 Use a micro-wave
44 On __ (without a buyer lined up)
47 Opposite of NNW
49 "Do __ say!" (2 wds.)

PUZZLE 68

ACROSS

1 Garfield, for one (2 wds.)
7 Taxis
11 Sewer access
12 Lands' End competitor (2 wds.)
13 __ the world (elated, 3 wds.)
14 Start for "violet" or "marine"
15 Star pitcher
16 Performs alone
18 Sneaky
19 Paving liquids
21 __ Wayne, Indiana
22 "Certainly!"
23 Knitter's unit
25 "Peter Pan" pooch
27 Comic Murphy
29 Was enamored of
32 Attain through work
34 Deceptive tricks
36 Gives a thumbs up to
39 Grasp firmly
41 Posy holder
42 Army officer (abbr.)
43 Cravat kin
45 ID with nine nos.
46 Belonging to them
48 Tied
50 "Maria __"
51 Patisserie purchases
52 Expresses disapproval
53 Subtract

DOWN

1 Flat as a __
2 Infiltrated
3 Even if, informally
4 Law officers
5 Cool and distant
6 Coating for non-stick cookware
7 250, to Cicero
8 Bohemian
9 Funny Milton
10 Influences
11 Trenches around castles
12 Very recently (2 wds.)
17 Unwritten
20 Before walk or long
24 __ Falls
26 Tel __
28 Messes up
30 Like a rubber band
31 Pudding, e.g.
33 Cut oneself while shaving
35 Forwards
36 Group of eight
37 Target competitor
38 Smooth and glossy
40 __ de León
44 Recited
47 Those holding power
49 It follows sigma

PUZZLE 69

ACROSS

1 Variety is the __ of life
6 Old sailor
10 Grandmas, to some
11 Broad-minded
14 __ forgiven (2 wds.)
15 Hard to pin down
16 Poker phrase (2 wds.)
17 In eager desire
18 Domestic animal
19 Actor Cariou
20 Ruin a hairdo
21 Bjorn of tennis
22 Phonograph disk
24 Was required (2 wds.)
25 "Little House on the __"
27 "I Am __"
30 Houston base-ballers
33 Exclamations
34 Totals (abbr.)
35 Cpl. or sgt.
37 Peugeot product
38 Matty of baseball
39 "__ Swell"
40 __ Davis of "Sex and the City"
42 Luxury hotel chain
43 Longed
44 "Sesame Street" regular
45 In the near future
46 Detection device

DOWN

1 Slow one
2 Golf great Arnold
3 Kind of skating (hyph.)
4 Abel's killer
5 Road curve
6 Farm towers
7 Snug as __ in a rug (2 wds.)
8 Guitar master __ Paul
9 Camera support
11 Notorious bootlegger (2 wds.)
12 Stave off
13 Unhand (2 wds.)
17 Subtle glow
20 Poet's dawn
21 Max of "The Beverly Hillbil-lies"
23 Accountants' initials
24 "Billboard" chart singles
26 Quartet follow-ing Q
27 Off-the-wall
28 Windy City hub
29 Shriver and Callas
31 Available (2 wds.)
32 Nova __
34 E.T., Alf, or Mork
36 __ space
38 __ extra cost (2 wds.)
39 TV host Banks
41 Box office sign (abbr.)
42 "...bells on __ toes"

PUZZLE 70

ACROSS

1 Two-door auto
6 Ran
10 Abilene's state
11 Beautiful Disney heroine
12 Attaches securely
13 Make __ for oneself (2 wds.)
14 Federal tax agcy.
15 Respond
17 Newsman Koppel
18 Honolulu neckwear
20 Alternative to Uber
21 Sets for "ER" and "Grey's Anatomy" (abbr.)
22 Doc for soldiers
24 Potting material
26 "I'm sorry!" (2 wds.)
28 Contemptuous expression
31 Cut
33 Judge's mallet
35 Bro's opposite
38 __ St. Laurent
40 Wine valley
41 Actress Lupino
42 Chewy competitor
44 "__ Hear a Waltz?" (2 wds.)
45 Scale members
47 Most ear-shattering
49 Car rental company
50 Undivided
51 Common contraction
52 Agreeable words

DOWN

1 Hopalong __
2 Canadian prov.
3 Utilizer
4 Discussion group
5 Compositions
6 Capitol Hill figure (abbr.)
7 Ancient philosopher
8 Fudd of cartoons
9 Legal documents
10 NBA great Abdul-Jabbar
11 __ cage
12 Movie
16 Corporate money managers (abbr.)
19 Bros, e.g.
23 Caribbean music genre
25 Thin
27 Jackknife, e.g.
29 Eluders
30 Rest
32 Tea maker
34 Café au __
35 Biblical mountain
36 Pagan images
37 Underworld figure
39 Tea biscuit
43 Double-play results
46 Rescue worker (abbr.)
48 Gambling cube

PUZZLE 71

ACROSS

1 Luxurious fur
6 "Look, up in the sky, it's __..." (2 wds.)
11 One ocean
12 More mellow
13 Part of the Pacific (3 wds.)
16 Fifth note
17 Actress Perlman
18 Martin or Jagger
19 Decides
21 As well
23 President after LBJ
24 Fan dancer Sally
26 Applies asphalt
28 Lean
30 Colder, as weather
31 Visitor
32 Shout
33 Business collaborative (abbr.)
34 Pig's dinner
36 Fawn's dad
40 Spanish girl (abbr.)
42 Gumbo pods
44 "__ Rita"
45 Hyannis Port sport (2 wds.)
48 "Believe It __!" (2 wds.)
49 Said
50 Provides food
51 Finalized

DOWN

1 Intrusive sort
2 Of legal age
3 Bridle piece
4 Bert of "Oz" fame
5 Bewitch
6 Operatic solos
7 Refrigerator drawer
8 Apple Store purchase
9 Engage a table in advance
10 One who fantasizes
11 "That __ unfair!" (2 wds.)
14 Kept
15 Dancer Miller et al.
20 Ladies of Spain (abbr.)
22 Milky-white gem
25 Tiny insects
27 Leather punches
28 Sports car feature
29 Talk given to a curfewbreaker
30 Scold
31 Essential point
32 Artist __ Ono
35 Artists' dwellings
37 Track down
38 Felt unwell
39 Top Olympic medal
41 Teenager's skin problem
43 "This suitcase weighs __!" (2 wds.)
46 Bricklayer's trough
47 Make an offer

PUZZLE 72

ACROSS

1 The opposite of labor (abbr.)
4 On the up-and-up
9 Leafy lunches
12 Saks Fifth __
14 Brunch favorite
15 Jeweler's measures
16 Resinous evergreens (2 wds.)
18 Bunny leap
19 "__ So Fine"
20 Pilots' approvals (hyph.)
21 Lonely
22 Chinese dynasty
23 Emery board
24 Nasal voice
26 Like many a superhero
27 Slippery critters
28 __ d'oeuvres
29 "Don't bet __!" (2 wds.)
30 Horse's hair
31 Health retreat
34 1812 outbreak
35 Printed handkerchiefs
37 Win over
39 Hollywood awards
40 Like a sauna
41 Moms' shout to fighting sibs (2 wds.)
42 Mexican misses (abbr.)
43 Draft org.

DOWN

1 Actress Van Doren
2 Valleys
3 Parable
4 Huron and Superior
5 Longoria and Gabor
6 Where Munich is (abbr.)
7 Owing money (3 wds.)
8 Taught privately
9 Junior-to-be, for short
10 Keeps in custody
11 Like Hercules
13 Home to "Baseball Tonight"
17 Cardiologist's reading (abbr.)
21 Mouth surrounders
22 Ovaltine ingredient
23 China's locale (2 wds.)
24 Rent payers
25 More unusual
26 Owner-occupied apartments
28 Chewbacca pal Solo
29 Has obligations
30 Astor and Martin
31 Breaks short
32 He loved Helen
33 Helper (abbr.)
35 Crimson Tide, familiarly
36 Service stripers (abbr.)
38 Have a meal

PUZZLE 73

ACROSS

1 Not plentiful
7 __ conditioner
10 "What a relief!" (2 wds.)
11 Say something more (2 wds.)
13 Singer Clark
14 __ Ark
15 Lode load
16 Soft cap
17 Roman robes
18 Complains
20 Grate cabbage
21 __ about (approximately, 2 wds.)
22 Nerd
24 Cantaloupe's kin (2 wds.)
29 Outer garments
30 Son of Leah
31 Like sci-fi fans, perhaps
33 Jimmy of "Superman"
34 Occupation
35 Where Botswana is (abbr.)
37 Mme., to a Spaniard
38 Waldorf, e.g.
39 Cheers
41 Apple tablets
42 Singer Dion
43 Matching china
44 Degrade

DOWN

1 Opera voice
2 Root for (2 wds.)
3 FBI investigator (abbr.)
4 Defeats
5 Pepsi, e.g.
6 Cheese from Holland
7 Old saying
8 "__ to Happen" (1936 George Raft film, 2 wds.)
9 Singer Diana
11 Patriotic song
12 Sign of a guest's arrival
15 "Oops!" (2 wds.)
19 Went before
20 Embroiders
22 June 6, 1944 (hyph.)
23 Dank
25 Rustics
26 Instructional units
27 Superintend
28 1492 ship
31 Feel one's way
32 Bother (2 wds.)
33 Toothbrush type (hyph.)
34 "Analyze __" (1999 film)
35 First four letters
36 Unencumbered
40 By way of

PUZZLE 74

ACROSS

1 Keystone figures
5 Bank customer units (abbr.)
10 Benedict Arnold's crime
13 Debutante's headwear
14 Autumn excursion
15 On __ the world (2 wds.)
16 Wayside stopovers
17 Hong Kong's continent
19 Sock part
20 Classic racecar, for short
21 Part of AARP (abbr.)
22 Taps lightly
23 Agitated (2 wds.)
25 "The Bridge over the River __"
27 Put back to zero
29 Indications
31 Alluring
32 Zest
34 Mischief-makers
36 Shriver et al.
39 Bear's young one
40 Born, in society pages
41 Baseball great Berra
42 "This is terrible!" (2 wds.)
43 Circular theater
45 Issue from
47 Better
48 Fire
49 Actor Hawke
50 "Mask" star

DOWN

1 Convention highlight (2 wds.)
2 Boat paddles
3 Greek consonant
4 Some mixers
5 "__ boy!"
6 AFL-__
7 Item on a sport fishing boat (2 wds.)
8 Scout unit
9 Vaults
10 Leg part
11 Angry speaker
12 "Untouchable" T-man
18 Moistens a stamp pad
21 Very top
22 Spaghetti sauce brand
24 Functions
26 Toupees
28 Printing error, informally
30 Knievel's forte
33 Certain woodwinds
34 Ridiculous
35 Earn
37 Ripened
38 Imitate
41 Knitting necessity
42 "Mother Pin a Rose __" (2 wds.)
44 Teacher's gp.
46 Fire aftermath

PUZZLE 75

ACROSS
1 Collect
6 Mine tunnel
11 Brunch side dish
12 City bird
14 Retired NBA star Shaq
15 Flying expense
16 Couturier Christian
17 School that's often K-6 (abbr.)
18 Gp. once headed by Heston
19 Keebler worker
20 Off-road vehicles (abbr.)
21 Agitate
22 "__ Fideles"
24 Trailblaze
25 Tennis's Nastase
26 Declare confidently
27 Worm, e.g.
28 Moistens the eye
30 Unconscious state
31 Roman 552
32 Timetable abbreviation
34 #6 on the phone
35 Pesci and Namath
36 Grab
37 Main meals
39 Tony winner LuPone
40 Cashes in
41 Phrase on a Bumblebee can (2 wds.)
42 Confirms attendance
43 Vice president before Harris

DOWN
1 Dwelling
2 "Thrilla in __"
3 High playing card (3 wds.)
4 Fly
5 Long-running comedy show (abbr.)
6 Cloak-and-dagger agents
7 Abuse
8 Sandy's sound
9 1986 NFL Hall of Fame inductee (2 wds.)
10 Scorching
12 Healing ointment
13 Dress in
17 Suffix for major
20 "Be that __ may..." (2 wds.)
21 Observed
23 Director Kazan
24 Super Bowl of 2023
26 MacGraw and Baba
27 Skinnier
28 Hallow
29 Dryer sheet's target
30 Nav. VIP
31 On-campus homes, for short
33 Nimble
35 Wrangler company
36 Rational
38 Reno's st.
39 Apple seed

PUZZLE 76

ACROSS

1 Weaker, as an excuse
6 Soup spoon
11 More aloof
12 Non-mechanical timekeeper
14 Mopes
15 Mentor's charge
16 Flat-bottomed boats
17 Viewed
18 151, Roman-style
19 Cul-de-___
20 Cry of regret
21 Perlman of "Cheers"
22 Quake
24 Brad of "Fight Club"
25 Had obligations
26 Parasites
27 Certain appliances
28 D.C.'s ___ Circle
30 DiCaprio et al.
31 Light carriages
32 Pronoun
34 Tide competitor
35 Some report card grades
36 Rdwys.
37 Harvesting
39 Spools
40 Banderas of "Shrek 2"
41 Japanese cartoon style
42 Conical tent
43 Author Ferber et al.

DOWN

1 Bonet and Hartman
2 Some Hondas
3 Candy bar ingredient (2 wds.)
4 Fun house shrieks
5 Four Monopoly cards (abbr.)
6 Entices
7 Unknown author (abbr.)
8 Banned bug spray (abbr.)
9 Franz Josef's principality
10 Baby bird of prey
12 Lance
13 Carrie Fisher character
17 Downhill vehicle
20 Some Monopoly properties (abbr.)
21 Puerto ___
23 "___ Made to Love Her" (Stevie Wonder, 2 wds.)
24 Gladys Knight and the ___
26 Oafs, informally
27 Become less strict
28 Muralist Rivera
29 "___ & Louise"
30 Zhivago's love
31 Magic lamp dweller
33 Hard letters for lispers
35 Patronize a restaurant
36 Wrest
38 Dad
39 Actress Charlotte ___

ACROSS

1 Oodles
6 Mothers, affectionately
11 Sweden's continent
13 In the least (2 wds.)
14 Navigates
15 Foster of "Panic Room"
16 Naval noncom
17 "Yes! Yes!," in Madrid (2 wds.)
19 Small amount
20 Crude fellows
22 Legs, slangily
24 Moisten
25 Bamboozled
27 Gmail alternative
29 Delay (2 wds.)
31 Rémy Martin product
34 Angry growl
36 Liquid-Plumr's competitor
37 Nintendo product introduced in 2006
39 Actor Hemsworth
41 Actress __ Rachel Wood
42 Spies (abbr.)
44 U.S. Pacific territory
46 Raised railroads
47 More cunning
49 Like some wood
51 Zero people (2 wds.)
52 Some inhabitants of India
53 Scout's rider
54 Strong point

DOWN

1 Famed guitarist (2 wds.)
2 Not where a player ought to be (3 wds.)
3 "The gloves __ off!"
4 Fawns' moms
5 Parsley bit
6 Milit. rank
7 __ bomb
8 Famed advertising center (2 wds.)
9 Supreme Court justice Samuel
10 Insomniac's need
12 Written assignment
16 Salt-water fishes
18 1998 Apple debut
21 Stitched together
23 Fitted with footwear
26 Consisting of two parts
28 Cruel person
30 Prudish person
32 Psychiatrist, perhaps
33 Jail inmates
35 Chuckle
37 "That __ so bad!"
38 Nanook's home
40 Callas of opera
43 Emitted
45 Provides workers
48 Antique car
50 Proofs of age (abbr.)

PUZZLE 78

ACROSS

1 Nanny ___
5 Mark Harmon TV show
9 Farmland unit
10 Cannon noise
11 Supporting vote
14 Jazz saxophonist Getz
15 One opposed
16 Smoked delicacy
17 Strike and rebound, as a ball
19 Colorful marble (hyph.)
21 Greediness
23 Confusion
24 Angler's trap
25 Deep mud
27 Organizer's challenge
28 "Sgt. Pepper" group
30 Radio choices
33 Actor Epps of "House"
34 Praying one's bench
37 Requests for Friskies
39 "Sweet Home ___"
41 Shows embarrassment
43 More foxlike
44 Texter's chuckle
45 Inning's six
47 Tax mos.
48 Naval off.
49 Nabisco cookie
50 Epic story
51 Pulled by doubts
52 Killed a dragon

DOWN

1 Garage container (2 wds.)
2 Series of eight musical notes
3 Where the Ark "docked"
4 Male voice range
5 Basketball gp.
6 Symphony figure
7 Small particle
8 Singer Kate ___
11 Headache relief brand
12 Toys on strings (hyph.)
13 Office "suits," informally
18 Wordless actor
20 Waterston and Donaldson
22 Jet-setter's farewell
26 Airline to Ben-Gurion (2 wds.)
28 German autos
29 Distinctive years
30 Stroll
31 Cantaloupe, e.g.
32 Sports infractions
34 Purchasing option for an eBay buyer
35 Come into view
36 Polish capital
38 Sprout
40 Couturier Bill ___
42 21st-century currency
46 Moses, to Gwyneth

PUZZLE 79

ACROSS
1 Seat
6 Wharton grads
10 Lady's top
11 Very high (2 wds.)
12 Police cordon
13 Textbook beginning, for short
14 "Only __"
15 Poke fun
17 Derby, e.g.
18 Ore vein
20 Malady
22 Related (to)
23 Disparaging
24 Tidy
25 Cherry middle
26 Put to flight
30 Works for
32 Foe of 007 (2 wds.)
33 Frat barrel (2 wds.)
36 Spoke
37 Tic-tac-toe line
38 Twice married
41 "Prelude __ Kiss" (2 wds.)
42 Prone (2 wds.)
44 Maintenance to a former spouse
46 Aired anew
47 Meats served with fried onions
48 Insult
49 Is in front

DOWN
1 Lady Bird Johnson's real first name
2 Swine
3 Mom's sis
4 "Got it!" (2 wds.)
5 It holds back soil (2 wds.)
6 "Spider-__"
7 "__ Beautiful Sea" (2 wds.)
8 Emanations
9 Detects
10 Burke or Shields
11 Control
12 Poet Thomas
16 Long cuts
19 Penetrate
21 Dweebs
23 Big shopping trip
27 Speakers
28 Workers' organizations
29 NBC morning show
31 Midwest rubber city
33 Wild pigs
34 Eject from school
35 Surplus
39 Writer Wiesel
40 Opera star
43 Knock lightly
45 Sm., __, and lg.

PUZZLE 80

ACROSS

1 Corn Belt state
5 44th U.S. president
10 Some shorts
13 French sculptor Auguste __
14 Signs up for
15 Using the exit
16 RBI, for one
17 Deli order
19 On an even __
20 Bro, e.g.
21 "Good heavens!" (2 wds.)
22 Remedy
23 Nautical nickname
25 Writer Bombeck
27 Lock, __, and barrel
29 Polite refusal (2 wds.)
32 Hawaiian wreaths
34 Just
35 Denim designer Strauss
38 Pats
40 Needing a doctor
42 Friends, en francais
43 Compass indication (abbr.)
44 Thailand's continent
45 Manly
47 Ordered by the judge
49 Toured on a ten-speed
50 Gratify fully
51 Playground chute
52 Green pods for soup

DOWN

1 "__ It Bad (And That Ain't Good)" (2 wds.)
2 Middle East export
3 __ corgi
4 Take for granted
5 Kin of assoc.
6 Place for paperbacks
7 Farewell, French-style
8 Gold digger
9 Corner formation
10 Good Queen __
11 Class clown's capers
12 Try to clutch (2 wds.)
18 Capital of Switzerland
21 Never before and never again
24 Elegant, in a way
26 Dads' mates
28 Legendary pirate captain
30 Spring blooms
31 Remedy
33 Declared (2 wds.)
35 Shepherd's charges
36 Internet messages
37 Lawrence of "Carol Burnett"
39 Snap off
41 __ Godiva
44 Soprano's operatic solo
46 Exalted poem
48 Middle (abbr.)

PUZZLE 81

ACROSS

1 Financial obligations
6 Pocketbook
9 Exasperated cry (2 wds.)
10 Start of a suggestion (2 wds.)
13 Big swallows
14 Tenders of livestock
16 Slump
17 Fasten securely
18 Red, e.g.
19 Certain soup legumes
22 Squeezing snakes
23 General's staffer
24 Praises highly
25 Scallionlike garnish
28 Square dancer's action
29 Underwear name
30 Tennis's Bjorn ___
31 Face shape
32 "M*A*S*H" role
35 Golf goal
36 NASA approvals (hyph.)
37 Listening requirement
39 Bai competitor
41 Taco topping
43 Came to terms
44 Sluggard
45 Always, of old
46 Sheriff's party

DOWN

1 Likes, slangily
2 Fifty-fifty
3 Protruding part
4 Tilt
5 Peter, Francis, etc. (abbr.)
6 South Pole's Admiral ___
7 In addition
8 Exits a building (2 wds.)
10 During
11 Roosters' mates
12 Tramples
15 Likely to talk back
17 Offers
20 Orange type
21 Neckwear
22 Boat used by Cleopatra
24 Prowl
25 Butchers' offerings
26 Castro's capital
27 Steaming (3 wds.)
28 Guernseys
30 ___ potato
32 Doughnut feature
33 Raises one's voice
34 Relaxes
36 Mimicker
38 Steak order
40 Sent or late start
41 Small taste
42 Hullabaloo

PUZZLE 82

ACROSS

1 Hence
5 "Casablanca" cafe
10 ___ girl (poster picture)
12 Temporary, as a position
14 Step
15 Ready for the rubbish heap (2 wds.)
17 Cereal tidbit
18 Uncloses
20 ___ Tin Tin
21 Submissions to eds.
22 Soggy areas
23 Furrier's item
24 Work hard and steadily
25 Knox or Dix
26 Following
28 Actress Palmer
29 Starting at
30 Male parents
31 Rowing team
32 Pence or Ditka
33 Timetable abbr.
36 Faux ___ (blunder)
37 Bank filler
38 Equip
39 "Rude Boy" singer
41 Talk ___ a minute (2 wds.)
43 Pattern
44 "___ Rock" (Chubby Checker hit)
45 Neck areas
46 Commencing with (2 wds.)

DOWN

1 ___ salts
2 Moreno et al.
3 Small, annoying insects
4 French affirmative
5 Caesar salad dressing ingre-dient (2 wds.)
6 Church pictures
7 Middles (abbr.)
8 Family reunion attend-ees
9 Noisy sleepers
11 Something to be solved
13 Jury's deci-sion, perhaps
16 Explosive trio
19 Indigent
23 Flower holders
24 Pack
25 Word in FDIC
26 Fearful
27 Brighten
28 Make brownies
30 Parlor seats
31 Lifesaving technique (abbr.)
32 Pooch's disease
33 Cuts a moustache
34 "Lord of the Rings" charac-ter Baggins
35 "The ___ Inno-cence" (Edith Wharton, 2 wds.)
37 Barbershop sound
40 Light ___ feather (2 wds.)
42 Soccer legend Hamm

PUZZLE 83

ACROSS

1 F followers
4 Treaty
8 London baby carriages
10 Writers
13 Barber's implement
14 Bing Crosby, for one
15 Fateful time for Caesar
16 "You're it!" game
17 Furtive whisper
18 Quill tip
19 Larger quantity
20 It's often served with hummus
21 Past the deadline (2 wds.)
23 Fixes a squeak
24 Conceit
25 Dr. of the rap world
26 College placement exams (abbr.)
28 Book-lending institution
32 Leveling device
33 Coniferous trees
34 Boundary
35 Domesticate
36 Calligraphy need
37 University VIP
38 Formal written communication
40 Sales goal
41 Continued, as a subscription
42 Tie up a stuffed turkey
43 Ridged wheel
44 Ocean craft (abbr.)

DOWN

1 Village green structure
2 Modern physicians' gps.
3 Tel Aviv's land (abbr.)
4 Cleanse thoroughly
5 From __ Z (2 wds.)
6 Less smooth
7 Adenoid's neighbor
8 Painting reproduction
9 Clock __ (2 wds.)
10 Not __ in the world (2 wds.)
11 Music notations
12 Spanish miss (abbr.)
16 Dorothy's pet
19 "People" and "Time," e.g. (abbr.)
22 "Hmmmm" (3 wds.)
23 Globes
25 Long dagger
26 Guise
27 Drawing a bead on
28 Like good wool skirts
29 Brand of hot dogs
30 Mob actions
31 Workout locales (abbr.)
32 After mob or shy
33 Office worker
37 Songwriter Bacharach
39 Inits. once seen at airports
40 Liquid measures (abbr.)

PUZZLE 84

ACROSS

1 Pen
5 Decompose
8 Rush off
10 "Finally!" (2 wds.)
13 Less difficult
14 Lose weight
15 Genetic info carrier (abbr.)
16 It spreads disease
18 Shipping weight
19 High-__
21 "The Maltese Falcon" author
24 Made queries
26 Dig up
27 Joshing
29 Curious Greek girl
32 Moola
36 "Up" voice star (2 wds.)
37 Grand Ole __
38 56, to Caesar
39 Snug as __ in a rug (2 wds.)
42 Swimmer's measure
43 Slanted
46 Reason
48 Showers ice pellets
49 "Gentleman __ Blondes"
50 Xmas mo.
51 Bus rider's hope

DOWN

1 Actor John
2 Onassis, informally
3 "Dharma & __"
4 "Jane __"
5 "66," e.g. (abbr.)
6 __ Glory
7 More tense
8 Sealy competitor
9 Help for walkers
10 Fashion designer Giorgio
11 Actress Kristin __ Thomas
12 10%
17 Strawberry __ pie
20 Cow groups
22 Darn socks
23 Mr. of cartoons
25 "Runaround Sue" singer
28 Coats with crumbs
29 Trappers' wares
30 Motrin alternative
31 Caught in the act
33 Buoy, as spirits
34 Very serious
35 Keyed up
40 Diamond figures, for short
41 Environmentalist Al
44 Golfer's prop
45 List-ending abbr.
47 Steeped beverage

PUZZLE 85

ACROSS
1 Withdraw
7 Painter Chagall
11 Maxim
13 Serious request
14 Eastern European country
15 Makes slender
17 Boat bosses (abbr.)
18 250, to Cicero
20 Draft status (hyph.)
21 Lipton product
22 Millinery merchants
24 Radiator's sound
25 Over yonder
27 "Yippee!"
28 Ambles
29 "Fresh Air" network
32 At __ (2 wds.)
33 TV brand
36 Less refined
38 Coffee container
39 Cathedral section
40 Place to be pampered
42 ...two peas in __ (2 wds.)
43 Retort
45 Hobbyist
47 Calendar's span
48 Marital dissolution
49 Ben & Jerry's competitor
50 The __ of despair

DOWN
1 Small herrings
2 Wears away gradually
3 Causes for pauses
4 Actress Longoria et al.
5 Family room
6 Actor Stoltz ("Mask")
7 AWOL pursuers
8 Parcel out
9 Comedic Carl
10 Photographing device
12 Single guy's abode (2 wds.)
16 Beauty contestant's banner
19 Singing birds
23 Dick Tracy's Trueheart
25 "__ the night before Christmas..."
26 Patriot Nathan's family
29 Chapel Hill's st.
30 Olive's beau
31 Grated harshly
33 Everett of "The Next Best Thing"
34 Stoop low
35 Previn and others
37 __ race
41 Between
42 Over
44 Parts of centuries (abbr.)
46 Fifth or Madison (abbr.)

PUZZLE 86

ACROSS

1 Laid bathroom floor
6 Most recent
12 Unwed
13 Speaker
14 "__, That's My Baby" (2 wds.)
15 Zipper substitute
16 Cpl. or sgt.
17 Whitened
19 Shade sources
21 "So's __ old man!"
22 "I feel like __ man!" (2 wds.)
24 Prom date, e.g.
29 Location
30 The "A" in U.S.A. (abbr.)
31 Driver using the left lane
34 Coffeehouse offering for web surfers
35 Club __ (resort)
37 Diplomat's need
39 Muffler's neighbor
44 __ mask
45 Wok recipe step (2 wds.)
46 President from Plains, Georgia
49 Ship's kitchen
50 Cling
51 Besmirches
52 Crazy

DOWN

1 Man's jewelry item (2 wds.)
2 Sheep-counter's complaint
3 Certain NFL linemen (abbr.)
4 Yale student
5 Kentucky __ (race)
6 Star-crossed __
7 Location
8 Powder ingredient
9 __ A Sketch
10 Angry
11 Walked on
12 Word in a 12/31 song title
18 Jeans brand
20 Fixes firmly
23 Director Craven
25 Sound in a cornfield
26 Forget to include
27 Tie again
28 Subterfuge
32 Dickinson and Post
33 Pence, e.g. (abbr.)
36 Window sticker
38 Grow weary
39 Price tickets
40 Eden man
41 At leisure
42 1970 Kinks hit
43 Fishing spot
47 Busy activity
48 Before sigma

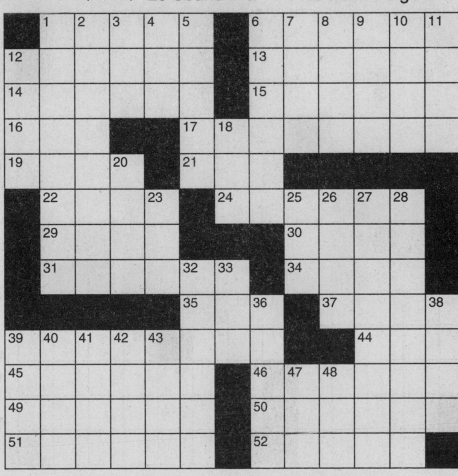

PUZZLE 87

ACROSS

1 Until now (2 wds.)
6 Shine
11 Clinton's vice president (2 wds.)
12 Leave alone (2 wds.)
13 __ bread
14 Comes into, as debt
16 Like thrift store merchandise
17 Alan of the silver screen
19 Certain sizes (abbr.)
20 Delighted sounds
21 Army camp
22 Italian make of car
23 MacGraw et al.
24 Popular jeans
25 Collected
28 Break down
29 Hertz or bucks start
30 Dundee's prey
31 Society gals
32 Actress __ Wray
35 Actor Linden
36 "Slamming Sammy"
37 Actress Theda
38 Traffic sign (hyph.)
40 Buffalo coin
42 Cook over charcoal
43 Trying experience
44 Cosmetician Lauder
45 Requires

DOWN

1 Cut roughly
2 Fairy tale monsters
3 Do a laundry job
4 Jackie's second husband
5 Demand the return of
6 Coast
7 __-Lease Act
8 And so on (abbr.)
9 Insulting
10 Legendary sea beauty
11 Water, in Barcelona
15 Grounded jets (abbr.)
18 Supposes
21 Police uniform color
22 Crumbly cheese
23 Electrically versatile
24 Tarries
25 Bring about
26 Ice chests
27 Beirut's nation
28 Canyon's reply
31 Sir Arthur Conan __
32 Forged
33 Locales
34 Everybody, down South
36 Garage __
37 Alphabetic quartet
39 Amusing person
41 Extreme anger

PUZZLE 88

ACROSS

1 Former White House family
7 Inc. relative
11 Showy flower
13 Kojak's first name
14 Wrapped dresses
15 Sprinted
17 Makes last
18 Big Apple sch.
20 Rank numerically
21 Envision
22 Hamlet's love
24 Graduation day VIPs
25 Keep in stitches
27 TV type
28 10th president
29 Friend (Fr.)
32 Like a cliché
33 Full theater abbr.
36 Scandinavian country
38 Bk. after Exodus
39 Words of approximation (2 wds.)
40 "__ So Fine"
42 Use toweling
43 Earth model
45 Storm trooper in action
47 Net pro Nastase
48 Rear part (2 wds.)
49 Actress Gwyn
50 Arrives at (2 wds.)

DOWN

1 Preoccupy
2 Lab vessel
3 Assents
4 Dairy sounds
5 Abby's twin
6 It might say "EXIT"
7 NBA position (abbr.)
8 Midwest hub
9 Summon back
10 Kind of justice
12 Shakespearean comedy (4 wds.)
16 Useless, as a battery
19 Worried
23 At this location
25 "__ boy!"
26 One of the Magi's gifts
29 "Lad: __" (2 wds.)
30 Arthur's magician
31 Arch support
33 Passes smoothly
34 Turn from sin
35 Cook too long
37 It merged with Exxon in 1999
41 Ragged tear
42 Cager Frazier
44 "Electric" swimmer
46 Fight

PUZZLE 89

ACROSS

1 Neckline shapes
5 "Common Sense" author
10 Loafed
12 Ornamented
14 Tank ship
15 Chemistry, history, etc.
16 Prone to drips
17 Montezuma, for one
18 Academic periods (abbr.)
20 Greek god of war
23 Medic's nickname
26 Abominable Snowman
28 Hayworth or Ora
29 Eludes
31 Restaurant table clearer
33 Phone or gram start
34 Tough fiber
36 Pulver, e.g. (abbr.)
37 Easy job
38 Govt. food-regulating agcy.
40 Money hoarder
43 Let
47 Innocuous pill
49 Little crown
50 They add up when you order more brewskis (2 wds.)
51 Bottled water brand
52 Holey cheese
53 Writer Stanley Gardner

DOWN

1 Stringed instrument
2 Falco or McClurg
3 Jazz great Fitzgerald
4 Searches for
5 Thrust the lower lip
6 Overdue debts
7 Engrave upon
8 Born as
9 Magazine employees (abbr.)
11 "...not a __ in the house" (2 wds.)
12 __ of thousands (2 wds.)
13 Group of 12 (abbr.)
19 Gym clothes material
21 Harrow's rival
22 Recites
23 Investigators (abbr.)
24 Range part
25 Squid dish
27 Some missiles
30 Portrays
32 Software fix
35 Current currencies, abroad
39 __ and kicking
41 They're blue on most maps
42 Subside
44 Lion's den
45 __-B (toothbrush brand)
46 Taper off
47 "Downton Abbey" network
48 Martial __

PUZZLE 90

ACROSS

1 300, to Cicero
4 Toy train sound
8 Cry like Lucy Ricardo
12 Exclamation of discovery
13 Momentary quiet
14 Faulkner's "As __ Dying" (2 wds.)
15 Sleep cycle (abbr.)
16 Stress
18 Rejuvenate
20 Directors
21 Zodiac sign
22 Milano of "Who's the Boss?"
24 Schreiber of "Salt"
25 Originate (from)
26 Actor Bean
28 Wet-eyed
32 Shreds
34 Art colony near Santa Fe
36 Football great Joe
39 Roald Dahl's Willy
40 Not good with (2 wds.)
41 Viewpoint
43 Light musical dramas
45 Eggy Christmas beverage
46 Compartment
47 Tops (2 wds.)
48 Explosive inits.
49 Out of port
50 Russia between 1917 and 1991 (abbr.)
51 Goose eggs

DOWN

1 Cattle enclosure
2 British "bye-bye"
3 More cozy
4 Crossword hints
5 Attila's followers
6 Out of date (2 wds.)
7 Grand __ Opry
8 Olympic gold medalist Simone
9 Jennifer Garner series
10 "A Fish Called __" (Kevin Kline film)
11 Caustic soap ingredients
17 Nursery __
19 Guns, as an engine
23 Sanctions
25 Agitated mood
27 Give a speech
29 "This suitcase weighs __!"
30 Met by chance (2 wds.)
31 John Lennon's wife (2 wds.)
33 Camera buff's collection
35 Serenaded (2 wds.)
36 Neck areas
37 "Easy on Me" singer
38 Tiffany Trump's mom
39 More intelligent
40 __ Raton
42 Pots and __
44 It follows sigma

PUZZLE 91

ACROSS

1 Procedure
7 Fair (hyph.)
11 "__ leap tall buildings..." (2 wds.)
12 Guitar sound
14 Looter
15 Escapes
17 Numbered hwy.
18 Concocted
20 Onion relative
21 Desires
23 Pucker formers
25 TV series set in Vegas
26 Mix slightly
28 Lose tautness
30 Most direct
32 Aromatic herb
35 Kringle or Kristofferson
38 Scand. country
39 Youngster's call
41 __ Lomond
43 Current with (2 wds.)
45 Supper, for one
47 Grade an egghead never gets
48 Songwriter Neil
50 Yacht basin
52 Carouse
53 Sunday hat
54 Thermometer units (abbr.)
55 Estimate

DOWN

1 Linger
2 Diminishes
3 Customer, to a lawyer
4 Mogul __ Turner
5 Ledger entry
6 Marine reef material
7 Church tower
8 Night bird
9 Author Bellow
10 Batting next (2 wds.)
13 Migratory birds
16 Rind
19 Undress
22 Intone
24 Canadian province (abbr.)
27 Enjoy Dickens
29 Computer keyboard key
31 Zoologist's subjects
32 Burden
33 Rodeo participant
34 Eaten away
36 Antiseptic substance
37 Play divisions
40 Brazilian dance
42 Warms
44 Basilica section
46 Asian country
49 Brewery cask
51 Healthcare professionals (abbr.)

PUZZLE 92

ACROSS

1 M.D.'s spot
5 Weeper's droplets
10 Altoid alternative (2 wds.)
12 Force to leave, as school
13 North American capital
14 Ignoramus
16 Regretful person
17 Damon or Dillon
19 Den, kitchen, etc. (abbr.)
20 Elect
21 Friends
22 Twerp's cousin
23 Sagan or Reiner
24 Apportions
25 "___, alligator!" (3 wds.)
28 Some Apple products
29 Rogers and Clark
30 Grow, as bread dough
31 Moore of "St. Elmo's Fire"
32 Busy worker in Apr.
35 Nonchoosy one's word
36 Boggs of baseball
37 Steer clear of
38 TV journalist Diane ___
40 Somewhat (2 wds.)
42 Kind of terrier
43 Oscar winner Kidman
44 Promotes extravagantly
45 Young woman

DOWN

1 Ask for a loan, informally (2 wds.)
2 Group of eight musicians
3 Hollywood notable
4 Bear's foot
5 Nomads' homes
6 Door out
7 Prone
8 Revise an article
9 More slender
10 Bull (Sp.)
11 Chevy model
15 Cooking measurements (abbr.)
18 Enticed
21 Reimburses
22 Moistens
23 Surrender territory
24 Polite request (2 wds.)
25 Popeye's favorite
26 Take the ___ out (2 wds.)
27 Phrase on a Chinese menu (2 wds.)
28 Retirement accounts (abbr.)
31 Mends argyles
32 Bedlam
33 Knitting maneuvers
34 Before (prefix)
36 "Wish You ___ Here"
37 Pound operators (abbr.)
39 Bark
41 Zero

PUZZLE 93

ACROSS

1 Mound
5 Causes dis-
   comfort
10 Prying tool
13 "Old MacDon-
   ald had __"
   (2 wds.)
14 1940 Hitch-
   cock classic
15 L.A.'s __ Drive
16 Police
   announce-
   ments (abbr.)
17 Diminutive
   suffix
19 Printer's need
20 Gdansk's
   locale (abbr.)
21 __ spumante
22 Figurine stone
23 Pittsburgh
   export
25 Razes
27 Cringed
29 Origins
31 Posters
35 Waiter's
   offering
36 Monogram pt.
38 Online chuckle
39 Puzzled
   comments
40 Accountants'
initials
41 Prudent
42 Heated gym
   location
44 Kind of grass-
   hopper
46 Rainy month,
   in Paris
47 Those who
   work for wages
48 Slowly leaks
49 Coffee con-
   tainers

DOWN

1 Limp along
2 Rams' mates
3 TV network
4 Walks ner-
vously
5 Hound's prey
6 "X-Files"
   object (abbr.)
7 Tire type
8 Vogues
9 Cigar emana-
   tion
10 Casino visi-
   tor's option
11 Transplant
12 Venomous
   reptile
18 Layer
21 Good many
   (2 wds.)
22 "Star Wars"
   character
24 Neutral color
26 Valet parker's
   wear
28 Licorice __
29 Conduct
   oneself
30 Take out a
   policy on
32 Slides
33 Respectful
   reply (2 wds.)
34 Flexible Flyers
35 Flat-topped
   hills
37 Oldest of the
   Hanson trio
40 Ripken, Sr.
   and Jr.
41 Ed of vaude-
   ville
43 Small bite
45 Singing syllable

PUZZLE 94

ACROSS
1 Flabbergasts
5 Nile's cont.
8 Name assumed by boxer Clay
11 Lemon's cousin
12 Town councilman
14 "SportsCenter" network
15 Sedan's four (2 wds.)
16 Italian wine
18 Brief burst of energy
19 Some mattresses
20 __ bopper
21 Leak out
22 Meat dishes
23 Thumbs-down vote
24 Went faster (2 wds.)
28 Saudi native
32 Native of Austin
33 Early harpsichord
35 Left Bank "thanks"
36 "Marie Antoinette" director Sofia
37 Type of rug
39 "Carrie" event
40 Wealthy (hyph.)
41 Alley
42 Thumbs-down votes
43 "Affirmative!"
44 Heart charts (abbr.)

DOWN
1 Baldwin and Guinness
2 Wants
3 NYC's __ State Building
4 Legislative body
5 Jai __
6 Fala's master's inits.
7 "Parted" water (2 wds.)
8 Quantity
9 David and King
10 "Meet Me __ Louis" (2 wds.)
12 Vaudeville attractions
13 Lassos
17 Short sleep
20 Wooden soldier, e.g.
22 Modern music genre
23 Cloister resident
24 Not mono
25 Pauline's woes
26 Make the honor roll
27 Delicate
28 Smartphone download
29 Fudge __ ice cream
30 Parka
31 Fit in
33 Han or Napoleon
34 Domesticates
35 Cut
36 Heartbreakers
38 Foot digit

PUZZLE 95

ACROSS

1 Gregarious
7 Pearl Harbor's locale
11 Chirping sound
13 Drescher or Lebowitz
14 Memoirist Maya
15 Rhythm
17 Bundle of paper
18 Compass letters
20 "___ for All Seasons"
(2 wds.)
21 Make a boo-boo
22 Disregard
24 Draft org.
25 Tolerate
27 Movie monogram
28 Latin dance
29 Give ___ go (2 wds.)
32 Brewery product
33 ___ Deco
36 Do not ___ (doorknob sign)
38 "Golly!"
39 Pet store brand
40 Quick touch
42 Wistful phrase (2 wds.)
43 Banana peels cause them
45 Large piece of farm equipment
47 One Great Lake
48 Prepared to propose
49 Four-sided figure (abbr.)
50 Places to bowl

DOWN

1 Glares
2 Possessors
3 New dad's handouts
4 News bit
5 NJ's ocean
6 Novelist Uris
7 Frequently, in verse
8 "It's been ___ pleasure!" (2 wds.)
9 Nail hitter
10 Empty luggage
12 Football position (2 wds.)
16 Informed about
19 Cheese chunk
23 Cogwheel
25 Rights gp.
26 ___ game
29 Lupino and Tarbell
30 Farmer
31 Seek to achieve
33 For a time
34 2012 candidate
35 Some sports coats
37 Subject under discussion
41 ___ fide
42 Brother of Cain
44 Group
46 Ott or Brooks

PUZZLE 96

ACROSS

1 Skills
5 LP alternatives
8 Zhivago's love
9 Half of a train sound
10 Cold as __
13 Somali super-model
14 Fiber plant
15 Head, informally
16 Go awry
18 100-year periods (abbr.)
19 Perfectly
20 Noncom, familiarly
21 Melancholy
22 Composer Duke
24 Hive creature
25 "__ whiz!"
26 Large dog (2 wds.)
30 Check cashers' needs (abbr.)
33 Innocent critters
34 Weird
36 Diva's song
37 Celestial body
38 Badminton divider
39 Chimney passage
40 Draft status (hyph.)
41 Hosp. figures
42 Dumbo's features
43 "America's __ Wanted"
44 Took action
45 Poker term

DOWN

1 Excuses heard from cons
2 Hotel chain name
3 Stenciled
4 Decaf brand
5 "Dancing with the Stars" winner Burke
6 Rounded roof
7 Drench
9 Iced
10 Unmoving
11 River of Africa
12 "Barnaby Jones" star
17 Groups of war ships
18 Wire enclosure
20 Respond to ragweed
23 Kindles
24 Rum cake
26 Pituitary __
27 Scarcer
28 Gives off, as light
29 Idiotic
30 __ patch (hyph.)
31 Least moist
32 Calm
35 Bakery emanation
37 Jai __
39 Provided dinner

PUZZLE 97

ACROSS

1 Former mlles.
5 The real __
10 50+ org.
11 Sudsier
13 Back portion
14 Home of the Raptors
15 Express displeasure
16 Actor Raymond __
17 Scout Carson
18 Tiny insect
19 Perfect
21 Certain plaids
24 Cut into cubes
28 Sings a lullaby
29 "I'm on it" (2 wds.)
30 __ makes waste
31 __ the bill (paying)
32 Skedaddle
34 Pop's wife
35 Clumsy fellow
38 Type of luck
39 Start of a wand-waving phrase
40 Slopes tool (2 wds.)
42 Helper (abbr.)
43 Removed from print
44 Command to a fly
45 Cut logs
46 Kal of "Designated Survivor"

DOWN

1 Pasta topper
2 Bernstein and Stokowski
3 Geological periods
4 April's season (abbr.)
5 Dudley or Roger
6 Auto dashboard item (2 wds.)
7 "__ Sharkey"
8 Pig's comment
9 Mythical monster
11 Ornamental nails
12 Decay
15 Incubate eggs
16 Vegetable drawers
20 Merry melody
22 Play-group attendees
23 Short story
25 Mounts (2 wds.)
26 "Honeymooners" role for Art Carney (2 wds.)
27 Religious doctrine
29 Where life begins
31 Known widely
33 Controlled
35 Psychedelic drug (abbr.)
36 Luau instruments, for short
37 __ monster (large lizard)
39 Arthur of tennis
41 Church seat
42 Cleo's snake

PUZZLE 98

ACROSS

1 Fall flowers
5 Snack
9 Poor review
12 "__ something I said?" (2 wds.)
13 Musical instrument
14 "Norma __"
15 Desertion
17 From alpha to __
19 Weasels' cousins
20 Ebb and neap
21 Writer Wiesel
22 "Born Free" feline
23 Tie-__
24 The girl
27 Textbook beginning, for short
29 Squelched (2 wds.)
31 Recent (prefix)
32 Opposite of conservative (abbr.)
35 Brooches
36 Shimmery mineral
37 Casaba, e.g.
38 Finished (2 wds.)
41 Additional
42 Month for Virgos
44 Racket or musket ending
45 "Othello" villain
46 Military group
47 He took the reins from HST
48 Distant
49 Part of NBA (abbr.)

DOWN

1 Gold-loving monarch
2 Apply
3 Irked
4 Hard and cold
5 __ Dame de Paris
6 Theater award
7 Chimney residue
8 Barnyard cluckers
9 Essential food category
10 Eeyore's creator (3 wds., abbr.)
11 Must (2 wds.)
16 Expresses sorrow
18 Transmission item
24 Not natural
25 Esteemed
26 Catch
28 Oily fruit
30 Very top
33 Delivery person way back when
34 Singer Streisand
36 Power source
37 Actress Streep
38 Thailand's continent
39 Table expander
40 Links org.
43 Ambulance worker (abbr.)

PUZZLE 99

ACROSS

1 Bush and Dern
7 Israeli airline (2 wds.)
11 Take issue with
12 Blended colors
14 Gardener's purchase
15 __ bowl
16 Nashville entertainment
17 "__ at the Races" (2 wds.)
19 Actress Longoria
20 Western state (abbr.)
21 Winter ground covering
22 Curl holder
23 Tic-tac-toe losing line
25 Washing __
27 Key player in basketball
29 Actress Loretta __
30 Handy one-volume reference
32 Med. gp.
33 Old phone feature
34 Summon
36 Jelly container
39 Longitude's opp.
40 Robin Cook book
41 Heavy mists
42 Observe, as laws
44 Military shoulder decoration
46 "__ Lucy" (2 wds.)
47 Invites to enter (2 wds.)
48 Last parts
49 Chinaware collection (2 wds.)

DOWN

1 Eccentric
2 Estimate
3 __-daisy
4 Friend of Winnie-the-Pooh
5 Korean, e.g.
6 Hardly ever
7 Handicrafts website
8 Humorous Costello
9 Lara Croft's portrayer (2 wds.)
10 Departing
13 Put a sari on
14 Haul
18 Not at home
21 Anon
22 Companion
24 Hockey rink shape
26 Anthracite
27 Resilient
28 Mexican dish
30 Stevenson of Illinois
31 Lunged towards (2 wds.)
35 Error
37 Contract negotiator
38 Letters after Q
40 So-so grades
41 Flurry
43 Thing that Netflix used to send
45 Alias letters

102   GREAT BIG CROSSWORDS

PUZZLE 100

ACROSS

1 Goofs off
6 Stolen goods
10 Baseball division
12 Late hour (2 wds., abbr.)
14 Orchard employee, perhaps (2 wds.)
17 "Lenore" author
18 Rind remover
19 Poet's prior
20 NBC comedy show, briefly
21 Fr. canonized women
22 Item for a piggy bank
23 Shuck
24 Football kick
25 Mint __
28 Lower female voices
29 Writer Bagnold
30 Singing voice
32 Bohemian
33 Progresso product
34 Sheep's comment
37 Born, in wedding announcements
38 Author Oscar
39 __ tide
40 With an insulting tone
43 Lions' homes
44 Fashions
45 "__ and the Tramp"
46 Singes

DOWN

1 Proceeds in a faltering way
2 Leek's relative
3 Devil's counterpart
4 Balsam __
5 Grabs quickly (2 wds.)
6 Home improvement chain
7 __ about (approximately, 2 wds.)
8 "__ the ramparts..."
9 Like some restaurant orders
11 Tiny insects
13 Italian wool
15 Difficult journey
16 Sublets
22 Some NCOs
23 Actress Lamarr
25 Simmons and Stapleton
26 False
27 Verbatim
28 Appearances
30 Metal fastener
31 Some German autos
33 Spacek of "Carrie"
34 "Ciao __!"
35 More fit
36 Bottomless pit
38 Hospital division
41 U.S. spy gp.
42 Supporting vote

PUZZLE 101

ACROSS

1 Expectant desire
5 Sail supports
10 "Reversible Errors" author Scott
11 Basketball's Shaq
12 Aggie or clearie
13 Tom Brokaw, e.g.
15 Taxing month
16 Classic racecar, for short
17 "Here __ again!" (2 wds.)
18 More substantial
20 Footnote abbr. (2 wds.)
21 Fireplace fragment
22 Belt's locale
25 Roof windows
26 Assign
29 "Get a Job" syllable
32 Midterm, e.g.
33 Scott competitor
35 TV regulators (abbr.)
36 Forest female
38 Watchmaker
39 Baseball's "Iron Horse"
41 Glum
42 Spanish title
43 Strives
44 Gaze fixedly
45 Abbr. on a mailroom stamp

DOWN

1 Common cheer
2 Circle the sun
3 Tadpole
4 Fleecy one
5 Protective ditch
6 __ Domini
7 Moment (abbr.)
8 Pacific vacation mecca
9 "Got Milk?," e.g.
10 Records
12 __ Cass
14 Actor's part
16 Contorted expression
19 Sweat for
20 Overhead railways
23 One son of Eve
24 Contents of Aladdin's cave
25 Badly lit
26 C followers
27 Surplus
28 Closet freshener
29 Looked happy
30 Nature walks
31 Unsigned (abbr.)
34 Ancient object
36 Fashion design name
37 Dreadful giant
40 Genetic letters
41 Ocean craft (abbr.)

PUZZLE 102

ACROSS

1 Having weapons
6 Heroic stories
11 Irksome
12 Hacienda feature
15 Sudden thrust
16 Lettuce variety
17 PC port
18 Bag
20 Glimpsed
21 Fractions of minutes (abbr.)
23 __-bitsy (tiny)
25 Norma or Charlotte
26 Dancer Miller et al.
28 Those with IOUs
30 "Otherwise..." (2 wds.)
32 Question
33 Friend (Sp.)
34 Seasoning
35 Ike's monogram
36 River in a movie title
38 Wise fellow
42 Lounge
44 Extra dry
46 Emeril's exclamation
47 Hoosier State
49 Enjoyed, slangily (2 wds.)
51 Ladybugs, e.g.
52 Intended
53 Clarinet player's needs
54 Heiress Hearst

DOWN

1 Excellent grade (2 wds.)
2 Employ again
3 CNN rival
4 Cardiologist's reading (abbr.)
5 Hides gray hairs
6 Throws out of an apartment
7 Dry measures
8 Intense anger
9 City vehicles
10 Scoffer
13 Like a dark, rainy day
14 De Mille of dance
19 "__ We Got Fun?"
22 Performed a carol
24 "__ Precious Love"
27 Cozy corner
29 Spider-Man's shooters
30 "Finished!" (2 wds.)
31 Defensive baseball player
32 Famed ship (abbr.)
33 Improvise (hyph.)
34 Annoy persistently
37 Abated
39 Miss __ (lose rhythm, 2 wds.)
40 Haggard
41 Containing nothing
43 Word on a local beer can
45 Soggy
48 Tavern drink
50 British beverage

PUZZLE 103

ACROSS

1 Hoarse
6 Naval officers (abbr.)
10 Higher berth
11 "Rock-a-bye baby on the ___..."
15 Grasps
16 Four Seasons hit (2 wds.)
17 Arrange
18 Peanut butter brand
19 Alan or Robert
20 Tidiest
22 No, to Beethoven
23 Onion's relative
24 Actress Ruby
25 Salt holder
28 Confront boldly
31 Midmorning time
32 TV's "___-Team" (2 wds.)
33 Assocs.
35 Sagged, as an unwatered plant
38 Shed fur
39 Manner
40 Verbalized
42 Like some ears
44 Tricky pitch
45 Qualm
46 Comedian Gracie
47 Body art, briefly
48 Disarrayed

DOWN

1 Toupees, slangily
2 Clothing protection
3 Church steeple
4 Coach's pre-game offering (2 wds.)
5 Many mos.
6 In danger (2 wds.)
7 Breeze
8 Ryan of romantic comedies
9 Enclosed car
12 "Holy ___!"
13 ___ but goodies
14 Heavenly body
18 Belittle
21 Ball-propping gadget
25 Treads heavily
26 Valiant
27 Fly fisherman
28 "___, matey!"
29 Company VIP
30 Vitamin container
32 Crafts
34 Rooster's walk
35 Resided
36 Titled Englishmen
37 Trashy taverns
41 Refuse permission
43 Tax preparer (abbr.)
44 A son-in-law of Jay on "Modern Family"

PUZZLE 104

ACROSS

1 Bridge "wild" cards
7 Be stinting
12 Fix a shoe again
13 Mahatma Gandhi's home
14 Throws in the towel (2 wds.)
15 Ear-splitting
16 Shoe width
17 CPR expert
18 Congeals
19 Elba of "Luther"
21 They go through loops
22 Price asked
23 Epps of "House"
25 Identical (4 wds.)
31 Electrified particles
32 "On the Waterfront" director Kazan
33 Asparagus piece
36 Shares a story
37 Frosting
38 Biol., e.g.
40 Dedicated poem
41 Accord's company
42 Kind of evergreen
44 Exterior
45 Startles
46 Gucci rival
47 Woven container

DOWN

1 Checked the fit of (2 wds.)
2 Turn about
3 Apply
4 Exodus leader
5 Damson
6 Between Aug. and Oct.
7 Heartfelt
8 Gentle hill
9 Jerk
10 Sprays water lightly
11 Disburses
14 State Farm rival
20 "Give __ rest!" (2 wds.)
21 Contemptuous sounds
23 Nose tickler
24 Peak (abbr.)
26 Honeymoon falls
27 Understand
28 #1 hit for John Legend (3 wds.)
29 Least spicy
30 Disburdener
33 Scrub
34 1492 ship
35 Came to a close
36 Turner and Louise
37 Waffle House competitor, for short
38 Picket-line crosser
39 Pepsi, e.g.
43 Provoke

PUZZLE 105

ACROSS
1 Irritates
7 Stallone title role
12 Lauren of "The Big Sleep"
13 TV sound
14 Hit the jackpot, e.g. (3 wds.)
16 That woman
17 James of jazz
18 Country bumpkin
20 Small amounts
24 Pagan images
27 Super suc-
cessful movie, e.g.
29 Olympic champ's award
30 Avoid
31 "Frasier" or "Laverne & Shirley" (hyph.)
34 Adjust back to zero
35 Viewpoints page (hyph.)
36 Fine fabric
38 __ fide
39 Golf goal
42 Movie archae-ologist (2 wds.)
47 Leap over
48 Trumpet's cousin
49 Pens
50 Flower parts

DOWN
1 "Amazing Race" network
2 Old time "have"
3 Real estate unit
4 Magical place
5 Antlered animal
6 Smooth
7 Crib toy
8 Subtle emana-tion
9 Caesar's 1,501
10 Certain pen
11 Impressed sound
15 News article
19 Nordic capital
20 Iowa town
21 Exclamations of discovery
22 Wait awhile
23 Proofreading instruction
24 "__ Tired" (2 wds.)
25 Actor Johnny __
26 Garfield's canine pal
28 Richard of "Chicago"
32 Rafts
33 Sawyer's buddy
37 Civil rights organization (abbr.)
38 Ill temper
40 Tennis player Kournikova
41 Film holder
42 Hospital tubes (abbr.)
43 Natalie Cole's father
44 Drunken offense (abbr.)
45 Actor Pesci
46 Wall and Sesame (abbr.)

PUZZLE 106

ACROSS

1 On the ball
7 Lawyers' group
11 __ Christi, Texas
12 Locales
14 Maintains law and order
15 Rummage
16 Flutters
17 Spanish girl (abbr.)
18 Computer keyboard key
19 Nintendo competitor
23 Snakelike fish
24 Web letters
26 Compass dir.
27 Eminent
31 Bankbook entry (abbr.)
32 Zeus's warrior daughter
33 Fit __ fiddle (2 wds.)
34 Pre-college exams (abbr.)
35 Prepare tea
39 "Sister Act" sisters
41 Small orchard
42 Church VIP
44 Medieval writers
46 Man the wheel
47 Get under control (2 wds.)
48 Academic periods (abbr.)
49 Four-door cars

DOWN

1 Frisky as __ (2 wds.)
2 Energy type
3 Multiple birth member
4 Bars that are scanned
5 It follows Mon.
6 Road curve
7 Remote
8 Showy flower
9 Renovate
10 Certain cat
13 "__ with a Kiss"
14 Army rank (abbr.)
19 Elves' boss
20 Octet number
21 Cements
22 "It's __ to Tell a Lie" (2 wds.)
25 Hamm et al.
27 Ladd and Keaton
28 Offensive remarks
29 Certain thea-tergoer
30 Audrey Hepburn film
36 __ Hood
37 Smooths (out)
38 Cager Unseld
40 "I __ to recall..."
41 NFL field
43 Monopoly foursome (abbr.)
44 Last-yr. students
45 Mediocre mark

PUZZLE 107

ACROSS

1 Reason for cake, informally
5 Suffix for a doctrine
8 Garbo of films
9 Engaged man
12 More unkind
13 Under a roof
14 Certain colony members
15 Canned food brand (2 wds.)
17 Melodic instruments
19 __ plaid
20 52, to Caesar
21 Summon publicly
23 Tel Aviv location (abbr.)
26 Shows disdain
28 Sampled food
31 Go astray
32 Swear
34 Military mail abbr.
35 Distinguished airmen
37 Difficult woman
39 Not year-round
43 "__ Almighty"
44 Go above and beyond
45 Busy months for CPAs
47 Memorizes
48 Satellites
49 Watch display (abbr.)
50 Apartment house, e.g. (abbr.)

DOWN

1 More like a spoiled tot
2 Dim-witted
3 Broke a fast
4 Fabric measure
5 Privy to (2 wds.)
6 Kilted clansman
7 Insignificant
8 Not fake
9 Boneless cuts of meat
10 "She Believes ___" (Kenny Rogers hit, 2 wds.)
11 Beautiful man
12 Shopping complexes
16 Soufflé ingredient
18 Apr.'s season
22 Rises
24 Lacking food
25 Rescinds
27 Pencil topper
29 Stubborn beast
30 Epsom __
33 South of Can.
36 "Fargo" filmmaker Joel or Ethan
38 Biblical king
39 Order to a stockbroker
40 Company head (abbr.)
41 Milit. school
42 Ewe's offspring
46 Candidate, for short

PUZZLE 108

ACROSS

1 Features of a walrus
6 Stitched together
10 Cigar residue
11 Charming et al.
15 Complains
16 Ancestry
17 Death notice, for short
18 In the ___ of time
19 Manhattan school (abbr.)
20 Common tree
21 Kitchenware
22 Drivers' aids
23 Magic Kingdom's neighbor
25 Ticonderoga and Dix
26 Business transaction
27 Easter flower
28 Pulls into port
30 Minds
32 Actress Fay ___
33 Clothes
35 Gobble up
37 Naval rank (abbr.)
38 ___ Jail (Monopoly square, 2 wds.)
39 "I cannot tell ___" (2 wds.)
40 Apply enamel again
42 Battle of the ___
43 Classic Wham-O toy
44 Sing gently
45 Deborah of "Beloved Infidel"
46 Early mornings

DOWN

1 California-Nevada lake
2 Still good
3 Garlicky seafood dish
4 Retained
5 Draft agcy.
6 Banana ___
7 Lindros and Heiden
8 Bat an eye
9 Ship's course (abbr.)
12 Sunny color (2 wds.)
13 Cairo's land
14 Dr. ___ (children's writer)
18 It's passed in class
21 Election figures (abbr.)
22 Burrowing varmint
24 Opposite of moist, in brownies
25 Bends the truth
27 Apple's apple, e.g.
28 Dopey, e.g.
29 Directive
31 Former Asian capital
33 Copier cartridge filler
34 Playful swimmer
36 Adolescents
38 Mock
39 Subtle glow
41 Question
42 Trio between A and E

PUZZLE 1

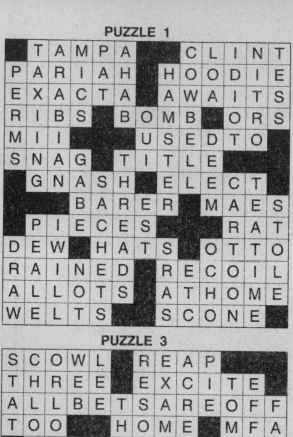

```
. T A M P A . . C L I N T
P A R I A H . H O O D I E
E X A C T A . A W A I T S
R I B S . B O M B . O R S
M I I . . . U S E D T O .
S N A G . T I T L E . . .
. G N A S H . E L E C T .
. . B A R E R . M A E S .
. P I E C E S . . R A T .
D E W . H A T S . O T T O
R A I N E D . R E C O I L
A L L O T S . A T H O M E
W E L T S . . S C O N E .
```

PUZZLE 2

```
. . I H A D . B I R D S .
O F F L I N E . K N E E L
P A R A S O L . S C U B A
T R O Y . L T D . I S U P
O I L . D D A Y . D E T S
U N I T E . S A M E . . .
T A C O M A . N A N C Y S
. . P O L S . S T R E P .
C L O P . I T C H . E L I
L O N I . S I R . F A L K
A R E N A . F O R E S E E
S N A G S . L O A N E R S
S A L S A . E K G S . . .
```

PUZZLE 3

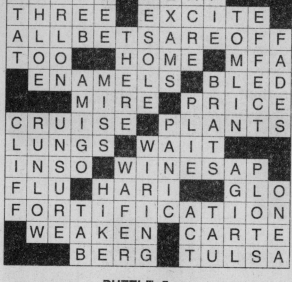

```
S C O W L . R E A P . . .
T H R E E . E X C I T E .
A L L B E T S A R E O F F
T O O . H O M E . M F A .
. E N A M E L S . B L E D
. . M I R E . P R I C E .
C R U I S E . P L A N T S
L U N G S . W A I T . . .
I N S O . W I N E S A P .
F L U . H A R I . G L O .
F O R T I F I C A T I O N
. W E A K E N . C A R T E
. . B E R G . T U L S A .
```

PUZZLE 4

```
A H E A D . S A L E M . .
H E I D I . T R E V I N O
O R E O S . Y O D E L E R
M O I . H A L S . L E W D
E N O S . S E E P . A C E
. . T A O S . H A G A R .
. D W A R F . M I S E R .
T A I N T . E E L S . . .
A P R . S I D S . T H R U
T H E O . F G H I . Y E P
E N T W I N E . S T E M S
R E A L T O R . A R N I E
. P S A T S . W Y A T T .
```

PUZZLE 5

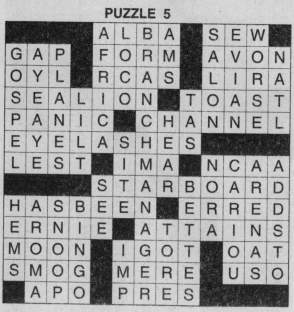

```
. . A L B A . S E W . . .
G A P . F O R M . A V O N
O Y L . R C A S . L I R A
S E A L I O N . T O A S T
P A N I C . C H A N N E L
E Y E L A S H E S . . . .
L E S T . I M A . N C A A
. . S T A R B O A R D . .
H A S B E E N . E R R E D
E R N I E . A T T A I N S
M O O N . I G O T . O A T
S M O G . M E R E . U S O
. A P O . P R E S . . . .
```

PUZZLE 6

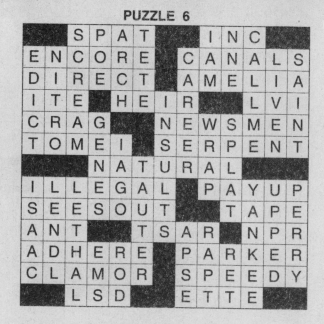

```
. S P A T . . I N C . . .
E N C O R E . C A N A L S
D I R E C T . A M E L I A
I T E . H E I R . L V I .
C R A G . N E W S M E N .
T O M E I . S E R P E N T
. N A T U R A L . . . . .
I L L E G A L . P A Y U P
S E E S O U T . T A P E .
A N T . T S A R . N P R .
A D H E R E . P A R K E R
C L A M O R . S P E E D Y
. L S D . E T T E . . . .
```

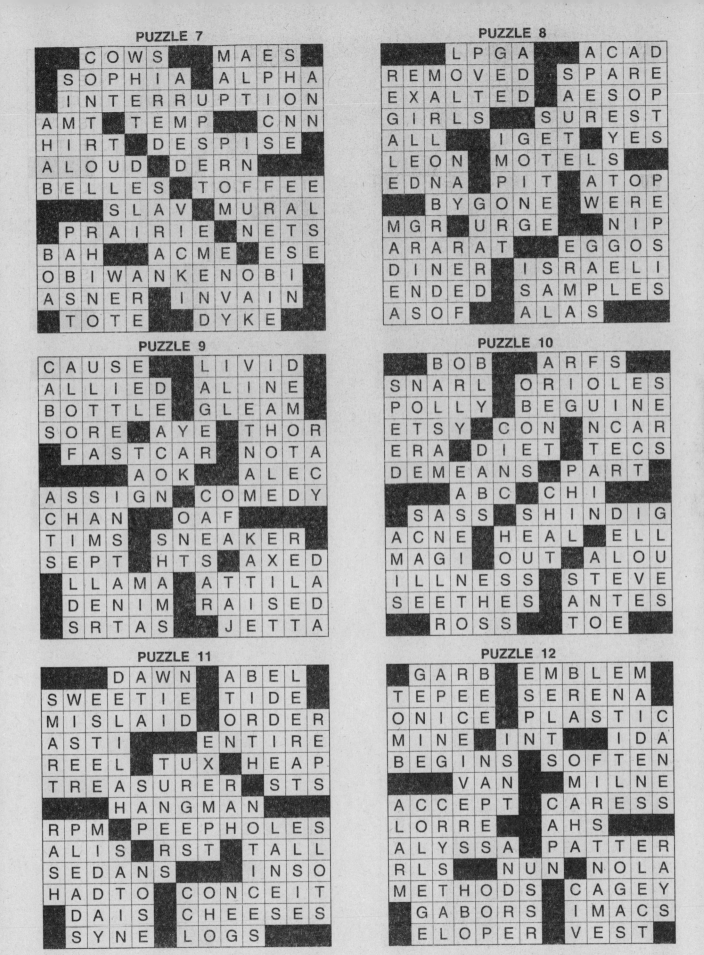

PUZZLE 7

C	O	W	S			M	A	E	S	
	S	O	P	H	I	A		A	L	P	H	A
	I	N	T	E	R	R	U	P	T	I	O	N
A	M	T		T	E	M	P			C	N	N
H	I	R	T		D	E	S	P	I	S	E	
A	L	O	U	D		D	E	R	N			
B	E	L	L	E	S		T	O	F	F	E	E
			S	L	A	V		M	U	R	A	L
	P	R	A	I	R	I	E		N	E	T	S
B	A	H			A	C	M	E		E	S	E
O	B	I	W	A	N	K	E	N	O	B	I	
A	S	N	E	R		I	N	V	A	I	N	
T	O	T	E			D	Y	K	E			

PUZZLE 8

		L	P	G	A			A	C	A	D	
R	E	M	O	V	E	D		S	P	A	R	E
E	X	A	L	T	E	D		A	E	S	O	P
G	I	R	L	S		S	U	R	E	S	T	
A	L	L		I	G	E	T		Y	E	S	
L	E	O	N		M	O	T	E	L	S		
E	D	N	A		P	I	T		A	T	O	P
		B	Y	G	O	N	E		W	E	R	E
M	G	R		U	R	G	E			N	I	P
A	R	A	R	A	T		E	G	G	O	S	
D	I	N	E	R		I	S	R	A	E	L	I
E	N	D	E	D		S	A	M	P	L	E	S
A	S	O	F			A	L	A	S			

PUZZLE 9

C	A	U	S	E		L	I	V	I	D	
A	L	L	I	E	D		A	L	I	N	E
B	O	T	T	L	E		G	L	E	A	M
S	O	R	E		A	Y	E		T	H	O	R
	F	A	S	T	C	A	R		N	O	T	A
		A	O	K			A	L	E	C	
A	S	S	I	G	N		C	O	M	E	D	Y
C	H	A	N		O	A	F				
T	I	M	S		S	N	E	A	K	E	R
S	E	P	T		H	T	S		A	X	E	D
	L	L	A	M	A		A	T	T	I	L	A
	D	E	N	I	M		R	A	I	S	E	D
S	R	T	A	S			J	E	T	T	A	

PUZZLE 10

		B	O	B		A	R	F	S	
S	N	A	R	L		O	R	I	O	L	E	S
P	O	L	L	Y		B	E	G	U	I	N	E
E	T	S	Y		C	O	N		N	C	A	R
E	R	A		D	I	E	T		T	E	C	S
D	E	M	E	A	N	S		P	A	R	T	
		A	B	C		C	H	I				
	S	A	S	S		S	H	I	N	D	I	G
A	C	N	E		H	E	A	L		E	L	L
M	A	G	I		O	U	T		A	L	O	U
I	L	L	N	E	S	S		S	T	E	V	E
S	E	E	T	H	E	S		A	N	T	E	S
	R	O	S	S			T	O	E			

PUZZLE 11

		D	A	W	N		A	B	E	L	
S	W	E	E	T	I	E		T	I	D	E
M	I	S	L	A	I	D		O	R	D	E	R
A	S	T	I			E	N	T	I	R	E
R	E	E	L		T	U	X		H	E	A	P
T	R	E	A	S	U	R	E	R		S	T	S
			H	A	N	G	M	A	N		
R	P	M		P	E	E	P	H	O	L	E	S
A	L	I	S		R	S	T		T	A	L	L
S	E	D	A	N	S			I	N	S	O	
H	A	D	T	O		C	O	N	C	E	I	T
	D	A	I	S		C	H	E	E	S	E	S
	S	Y	N	E		L	O	G	S			

PUZZLE 12

	G	A	R	B		E	M	B	L	E	M	
T	E	P	E	E		S	E	R	E	N	A	
O	N	I	C	E		P	L	A	S	T	I	C
M	I	N	E		I	N	T			I	D	A
B	E	G	I	N	S		S	O	F	T	E	N
			V	A	N		M	I	L	N	E	
A	C	C	E	P	T		C	A	R	E	S	S
L	O	R	R	E			A	H	S			
A	L	Y	S	S	A		P	A	T	T	E	R
R	L	S		N	U	N		N	O	L	A	
M	E	T	H	O	D	S		C	A	G	E	Y
	G	A	B	O	R	S		I	M	A	C	S
E	L	O	P	E	R		V	E	S	T		

PUZZLE 13

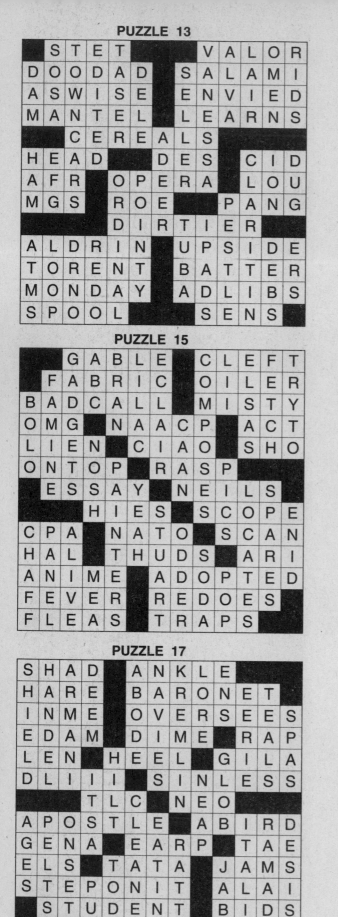

```
. S T E T . . V A L O R
D O O D A D . S A L A M I
A S W I S E . E N V I E D
M A N T E L . L E A R N S
. . C E R E A L S . . . .
H E A D . . D E S . C I D
A F R . O P E R A . L O U
M G S . R O E . . P A N G
. . . D I R T I E R . . .
A L D R I N . U P S I D E
T O R E N T . B A T T E R
M O N D A Y . A D L I B S
S P O O L . . S E N S . .
```

PUZZLE 14

```
. H O E D . . . . C F O
. T A B O O . P U S H U P
S E R E N E . O N T I M E
C A D S . S I T U A T E D
A R C E D . R O M P . . .
M O O . N O R M . L A S .
P O R T A L . A G E N T S
. M E H . Y M C A . D R E
. . E M M A . B R I A N .
L O L L I P O P . A R I D
A L U M N I . A B B O T S
C A N A D A . P A I N S .
E F G . . . . A D D S . .
```

PUZZLE 15

```
. G A B L E . C L E F T
. F A B R I C . O I L E R
B A D C A L L . M I S T Y
O M G . N A A C P . A C T
L I E N . C I A O . S H O
O N T O P . R A S P . . .
. E S S A Y . N E I L S .
. . H I E S . S C O P E .
C P A . N A T O . S C A N
H A L . T H U D S . A R I
A N I M E . A D O P T E D
F E V E R . R E D O E S .
F L E A S . T R A P S .
```

PUZZLE 16

```
. R A S P S . . A T T A
. H O T T E A . L L O Y D
C O M M I T S . E L O P E
A V A . R E H A B . T O P
R E N T . S E G A . H S T
A L C O A . S E N T . . .
. S E T U P . D O O R S .
. . O T I S . N A O M I .
E A T . U N I T . D Y E D
L E O . M S N B C . A L E
M I X I N . G O R I L L A
S O I L S . E N A C T S .
T U C K . D E W E Y . .
```

PUZZLE 17

```
S H A D . A N K L E . .
H A R E . B A R O N E T .
I N M E . O V E R S E E S
E D A M . D I M E . R A P
L E N . H E E L . G I L A
D L I I I . S I N L E S S
. . T L C . N E O . . .
A P O S T L E . A B I R D
G E N A . E A R P . T A E
E L S . T A T A . J A M S
S T E P O N I T . A L A I
. S T U D E N T . B I D S
. . P O R G Y . S C A T
```

PUZZLE 18

```
. D I T T O . C A R P S
M E M O I R . S U T U R E
A L P A C A . P I L L O W
M E L D . L O I S . E M S
A T A . . F R I A R S .
S E N D . S T I N G . .
. S T O R E . T E E U P
. . P O E T S . D R A B
. C R E C H E . . C L I
A R E . K E N O . T H A T
B I N D E R . C H O I C E
R E T I R E . T A N N E R
A S S E S . S W I S S .
```

114   **GREAT BIG CROSSWORDS**

PUZZLE 19

```
S A R G E . . R E A R . .
A D I O S . A I S L E S .
L E G O S . P O P S T A R
E L I . . H E D Y . R Y E
M E D I C A R E . B A S E
. . . N O T S . C L I N K
A W H I L E . C H I N O S
B E A T S . F O A M . .
L A D S . S L U R P I N G
E V A . S H I P . . R E L
R E F U G E E . B R A V O
. S I T T E R . I N N E R
. T E S T . . D A I R Y
```

PUZZLE 20

```
. G E I S H A . . R E S T
F O N D U E S . B E T T E
L E A S E R S . A C H E D
U S B . R O U N D . E N D
F O L D . D R U G . L O Y
F U E L S . E M I T . .
. T R I N I . B R A G S
. . I O T A . L U R E D
O F A . C O T E . T E R I
N O T . A N T S Y . E V A
T U L I P . E T E R N A L
A L A N S . N E A T E N S
P S S T . . D E S E R T
```

PUZZLE 21

```
. . B E T . . M E D A L
. T U R E E N . S E E T O
R I C A R D O . S E A T S
I C K . M I A S . L Y E
S T E W . T H I R S T S
K A Y A K . S L O P . .
S C E N E S . L O A F E D
. . D R A W . F R I A R
. C H A R L I E . S A R I
S H E . E L L A . N N E
L I M E S . D E F A C E D
A T A L L . E V A D E R
P A N K Y . . R O E
```

PUZZLE 22

```
E M B O S S . S A S H
M A R P L E . W I L E S
R E T A P E D . A D O R N
A R T S . P E E K A B O O
H A H . I T R Y . S S W
S L A T S . S E G A .
. D U E T O . S O F A R
. . D O U G . A B N E R
B A A . R O I L . T V A
A S S E S S O R . A H E M
B I B L E . B E A C O N S
A D I M E . E N D I N G
. E G O S . R E D D Y E
```

PUZZLE 23

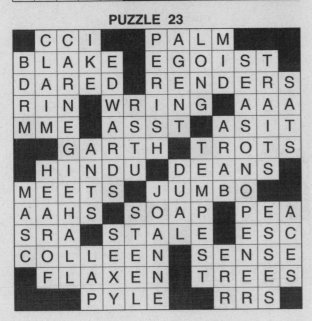

```
. C C I . P A L M
B L A K E . E G O I S T
D A R E D . R E N D E R S
R I N . W R I N G . A A A
M M E . A S S T . A S I T
. . G A R T H . T R O T S
. H I N D U . D E A N S
M E E T S . J U M B O
A A H S . S O A P . P E A
S R A . S T A L E . E S C
C O L L E E N . S E N S E
. F L A X E N . T R E E S
. . P Y L E . . R R S
```

PUZZLE 24

```
A M B U S H . C A N A L
B E A M E D . D R O V E
R A I S E T H E R O O F
P A N T . D V I . I N I T
E D I E . . S A V E D
R E N D . R O S I E
M S G . C E D E D . S I S
. . E L V E S . S U N S
. C U R V E . . P I T T
C O N N . R O D . R T E S
A C C E L E R A T I O N
L O U S E . E M B E R S
M A T T S . S P A R S E
```

PUZZLE 25

```
APTS    BOAST
 RHYTHM MOCHA
CROPPER WHEAT
RATE EBBS  TWA
UNO  ODIE HALS
EGGON  GROOM
TERROR TARIFF
  ACRES HANOI
RIPA  ACLU  ORR
UGH  FLOE APBS
SLIER  RAINHAT
TONKA  ERODED
SOGGY   NINE
```

PUZZLE 26

```
   EATS   OTTER
ROADMAP  LAURA
ORIGAMI  ELBOW
OGRE  PKG  LADE
TAO  KAEL  USER
  NUDE  DILL
  STEER BOARD
  MNOP  CHOO
BITE  MACK  SGT
AREA  ARR  TILE
DIANA  TARHEEL
ASSOC  ENLARGE
THERE   DESI
```

PUZZLE 27

```
 AMFM  SNEAKS
SHOOT  KIMMEL
LOTUS  ACTONE
AMER  ITE  KNEE
BELT  BERG  ETA
   ELMS  UDDER
AGREES  LLOYDS
BEANS  KILN
BOY  SEEM  ABOW
ARMS  LEA  TACO
 GOOFUP  AIMTO
 INSIDE  ROBES
 ADORER  KNIT
```

PUZZLE 28

```
  HAWN    MIAMI
ROADHOG  POPIN
ANDMORE  SNARE
NEA  AMOS  SCAR
TOGS  AROW  HGT
 FOES  GOATEE
  LICENSE
 MILDEW  HANS
SAM  SOBS  MOTE
PIPE  SUED  GOV
IDOLS  SMUGGLE
RESET  HIPPIES
ENEMY   SEAN
```

PUZZLE 29

```
  BROS   REVS
RECEIVE  TRIPE
USEDCARDEALER
STL  ALIE  SLAM
THIS  SAFE  AKA
YENTA  LOAN
 REELS  GRIMM
  RUTS  SNEER
FOB  MAIN  OSLO
IRON  RCAS  SOD
NEWYORKMINUTE
NOISY  LEDUPTO
 SEES  EDEN
```

PUZZLE 30

```
 SPEDUP    SEA
 HOARSE  BANDS
 ONRAMP  IRONS
LET  PCS  GROAN
ABITE    SWATS
NOAH  TAPIN
EXCESSBAGGAGE
  ROKER  EVEL
 FLAWS   EDITS
OLIVE  CPL  ALA
LONER  PUERTO
GWENS  ARGUES
ANN   SLYEST
```

PUZZLE 31

```
  M A E   E M M A S
T E S S   L E A P E R S
O D I E   A R R O G A N T
M I A   C I I I   A B E E
B A N D A N N A     B E L
    O R E O   M A I Z E
  S L E D S   H A S T Y
S P U R S   G A G A
O R G     T R U M P E T S
M E O W   R O N A   L O P
E A S E S O U T   A L L A
  D I S P O S E   H I L T
    T Y P E D   A S S
```

PUZZLE 32

```
A M F M     P U S H E D
H E R O I C   I N M A T E
A M A N D A   G L A N C E
S E N I O R   S A L K
    C L A M   C L E A N
S R T A   M O D E   R I O
A A H   R E W E D   E D S
I V E   E L E V   D D A Y
L I S P S   R I P E
    T A P E   S L A Y E D
O L I V I A   E U R E K A
D I N E R S   S M I L E R
D E G R E E     E L S E
```

PUZZLE 33

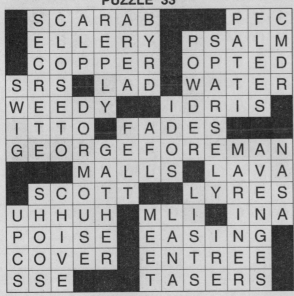

```
  S C A R A B   P F C
  E L L E R Y P S A L M
  C O P P E R O P T E D
S R S   L A D   W A T E R
W E E D Y   I D R I S
I T T O   F A D E S
G E O R G E F O R E M A N
    M A L L S   L A V A
  S C O T T   L Y R E S
U H H U H   M L I   I N A
P O I S E   E A S I N G
C O V E R   E N T R E E
S S E     T A S E R S
```

PUZZLE 34

```
  M A D A M   A F L A T
D I V I D E   N O T C H
E L O P E D   J O S H U A
N E W S   I P O D   I N D
S S S   O A H U   R E D D
      O N T O   M O V E S
    A P P L E B U T T E R
S T O R Y   I N N S
W A R Y   M A E S   P M S
A L T   P I S A   E L I E
M O I N E S   R E N A M E
  S O R E S   T I D I E R
S N A K Y   H O S T S
```

PUZZLE 35

```
A F A R   W O M E N
D I D N T   I N A S E C
A R O S E   L E C T U R E
Y E P   M E S A S   T O A
S S T   P R O M   T R O T
    B U R N   D I A N A
C E D A R S   W A L L S T
O M A H A   D I V E
W I G S   H O P I   A R M
E N G   K A R E N   R E O
D E E P E N S   C I T E D
  M R H Y D E   I L I K E
  S I S S Y   L E S S
```

PUZZLE 36

```
K A T I E   L E A R
E L U D E   S I S T E R
A L T A R   E M P O W E R
N A T   P E O N   R A E
U N I F O R M S   M O P E
    R U E S   F A T E D
A W A I T S   T I M E R S
F A S T S   S O D A
I N S O   A C R O S T I C
S T U   S M E E   R K O
H A M E L I N   S A U N A
  D E M I S E   A S C O T
  S S T S   C H E W S
```

PUZZLE 37

	G	P	S				R	I	P	E	R
	D	O	R	E	M	I		A	M	I	L	E
S	E	R	E	N	E	R		H	A	L	O	S
O	C	D		T	I	K	I		A	P	T	
W	O	O	L		N	E	S	C	A	F	E	
E	D	N	A	S		D	I	A	Z			
D	E	S	I	L	U		T	A	T	T	L	E
		R	A	N	D		N	E	I	L	S	
	P	A	S	T	U	R	E		C	E	O	S
B	I	B		M	A	X	I		D	Y	E	
A	N	A	M	E		M	E	T	H	O	D	S
A	C	T	O	R		S	C	R	E	W	S	
S	H	E	D	S			Y	E	N		

PUZZLE 38

N	A	A	C	P		P	E	P	S	I	
Y	E	L	P	S		E	L	A	P	S	E
P	I	V	O	T		A	B	R	A	H	A	M
D	O	I		A	L	O	T		M	R	I	
	U	N	S	C	R	E	W		B	A	N	S
		H	O	O	D		S	L	E	E	T	
E	N	F	O	L	D		S	C	A	L	D	S
W	I	L	E	S		C	H	U	M		
E	G	O	S		C	L	E	M	E	N	S	
R	H	O		C	H	A	D		O	I	L	
S	T	R	I	V	E	S		A	O	R	T	A
	S	E	R	I	E	S		F	U	S	E	D
		D	A	I	R	Y		T	R	E	S	S

PUZZLE 39

L	A	W	S		S	T	E	M		S	A	T
E	C	R	U		E	R	L	E		P	R	O
A	C	I	D		R	O	O	S	T	I	N	G
D	O	G	S		E	U	P	H	O	R	I	A
T	U	G		A	N	T	E		D	O	E	S
O	N	L	I	N	E		S	R	A		
	T	E	N	N			E	T	S	Y		
		V	E	E		M	E	E	T	U	P	
V	I	S	A		A	S	O	F		A	C	E
E	C	L	I	P	S	E	D		B	R	A	T
N	O	O	N	T	I	M	E		E	T	T	A
T	N	T		A	L	I	S		E	L	A	L
S	S	S		S	Y	S	T		P	E	N	S

PUZZLE 40

S	O	L	V	E		B	L	I	S	S	
C	R	E	A	K		E	A	R	A	C	H	E
A	I	S	L	E		G	N	A	S	H	E	S
L	O	S	E		V	I	C		S	L	A	P
P	L	O	T	L	I	N	E		E	E	L	Y
S	E	N		M	S	N		T	S	P	S	
		N	E	E	D	Y			
N	A	T	O		R	E	P		A	D	A
S	O	B	E		A	S	C	E	N	D	E	D
O	B	O	E		G	L	O		O	R	S	O
P	L	A	T	E	A	U		S	L	I	E	R
H	E	R	E	T	I	C		S	T	A	R	E
		D	R	A	N	K		T	E	N	T	S

PUZZLE 41

	S	H	E	M		H	U	F	F	S
T	A	U	R	U	S		S	M	E	L	L
B	R	I	T	I	S	H		T	A	N	Y	A
L	I	L		K	I	A	S		C	N	N
A	C	O	W		C	R	E	S	C	E	N	T
S	I	R	E	N		P	E	T	A		
E	A	S	I	E	R		D	A	R	N	I	T
		R	O	U	T		R	A	I	N	Y
G	O	O	D	N	E	W	S		T	B	S	P
E	L	M		R	I	P	A		B	I	O
A	D	E	P	T		G	E	R	A	L	D	S
R	I	G	I	D		S	E	T	T	E	E	
S	E	A	T	S			D	Y	E	S	

PUZZLE 42

	A	T	O	P			G	U	I	L	T
S	T	R	O	K	E	D		I	N	D	I	A
T	H	A	T	S	A	L	L	F	O	L	K	S
O	R	B	S		R	I	O	T		E	E	K
V	I	I		S	L	I	D		U	R	N	S
E	V	A	D	E		I	G	O	T		
	E	N	E	M	Y		E	N	A	C	T
		L	I	M	P		C	H	O	I	R
B	A	B	E		C	A	F	E		U	P	A
O	D	E		B	A	L	I		A	N	T	I
M	A	L	T	E	S	E	F	A	L	C	O	N
B	P	L	U	S		D	E	R	B	I	E	S
S	T	A	B	S		S	E	A	L		

PUZZLE 43

```
  B A K E S   G R O A N
P E D A L S   R A D I O
A L D R I N   E V E R S O
S O L E S   S E E S R E D
O W E N   M O N   A G O
      I F F Y   F R I A R
A M A N D A   G L A D Y S
L U N A R   L E O N
A S I   D O M   S L I P
R E S T S U P   L A U R A
M U T A T E   R E C T O R
  M O R A L   L I K E N S
  S N A G S   S A S S Y
```

PUZZLE 44

```
  S P O T   A J A X
S P A R E   M E L O D I C
N I C E R   E N D O R S E
A R I   R A N G E   O L E
P A N D A S   A N N I E S
S L O U C H     A D S
      E E E   H O N
    M G T   E N A B L E
S A L O M E   R E S E A L
C P O   E S S A Y   T B A
A L B E R T A   E G R E T
N E E D L E R   A T A L E
      S E E K   R O Y S
```

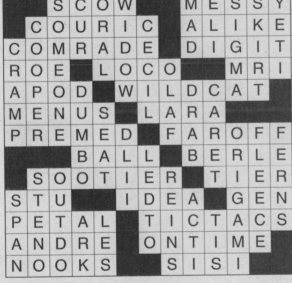

PUZZLE 45

```
    S C O W   M E S S Y
  C O U R I C   A L I K E
C O M R A D E   D I G I T
R O E   L O C O   M R I
A P O D   W I L D C A T
M E N U S   L A R A
P R E M E D   F A R O F F
    B A L L   B E R L E
  S O O T I E R   T I E R
S T U   I D E A   G E N
P E T A L   T I C T A C S
A N D R E   O N T I M E
N O O K S   S I S I
```

PUZZLE 46

```
S C R E W   G N A R L
T H E M E   B O Y H O O D
R A N T S   R I C O T T A
U S A   T O O N   L A I R
T E M P E R A   E T O N
  D E G R A D E   E N S
    S N L   X V I
S E C   B A C A R D I
K N O B   H O N K I N G
I T L L   G E N E   A V A
M I L I T I A   S E N O R
S T I P E N D   S H A K Y
  Y E S E S   A S S E S
```

PUZZLE 47

```
    T Y P O   T I D A L
A D J O U R N   S N A R E
G O E S M A D   P A N D A
C O T S   D E S   P E E P
Y D S   P A C K   I S N T
  L E T A   K I L N
  E T H I C   D I C E D
    A D O S   O H N O
R A F T   L A W N   A N T
O T I S   A C H   S C A R
A B E A T   R I S O T T O
M A R L O   E L A P S E D
S T Y L E   D E M S
```

PUZZLE 48

```
A R A B I A   S O L O
B A L A N C E   O N A N
A N T E N N A   S T U F F
S O A R   E R R   A R I A
E U R   L E O P A R D
S T S   B E G I N   S E E
    L A R G E
N E T   O V E N S   P H I
D I S O B E Y   H A N
A L E S   S T P   L O S S
K E T C H   E A S I E S T
  E S A U   A M I A B L E
  N E R D   S T R E E P
```

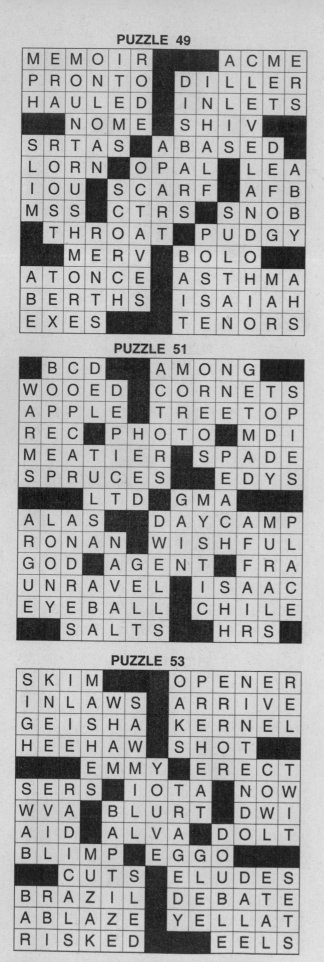

PUZZLE 49

```
M E M O I R   │ │   A C M E
P R O N T O   │ D I L L E R
H A U L E D   │ I N L E T S
  │ N O M E   │ S H I V   │
S R T A S   │ A B A S E D
L O R N   │ O P A L   L E A
I O U   │ S C A R F   A F B
M S S   │ C T R S   S N O B
  │ T H R O A T   P U D G Y
  │ M E R V   B O L O
A T O N C E   A S T H M A
B E R T H S   I S A I A H
E X E S   │   T E N O R S
```

PUZZLE 50

```
│ S P A M   A L D E R S │
S A U C E   S E A S O N
E B B E D   P E R T A I N
W E L D   D I R K   N C O
S R I   F U R Y   Y O K O
  │ C H I D E   W A K E N
  P S A T S   P A R E R
H E E L S   H E I D I
E A R L   M I S T   S U B
M C V   L O G O   E L M O
P H A R A O H   C L A P S
E N A M E L   P I N E S
S T E A D Y   L A D D
```

PUZZLE 51

```
│ B C D   A M O N G │
W O O E D   C O R N E T S
A P P L E   T R E E T O P
R E C   P H O T O   M D I
M E A T I E R   S P A D E
S P R U C E S   E D Y S
    L T D   G M A
A L A S   D A Y C A M P
R O N A N   W I S H F U L
G O D   A G E N T   F R A
U N R A V E L   I S A A C
E Y E B A L L   C H I L E
  S A L T S   H R S │
```

PUZZLE 52

```
S C A L D   R E L I C
N U D G E   O R A T O R
A R I E L   S O D A P O P
C I O   A S I D E   I W O
K O S   W H E E   O L E S
  P A I R   I V O R Y
A D O R N   G N A T S
W R I T E   W A I L
H O S S   M E L T   W E T
I M A   S I N A I   R T E
G A R L A N D   A L O H A
S M O K E Y   T O N E S
  S L E D S   E A G L E
```

PUZZLE 53

```
S K I M   O P E N E R
I N L A W S   A R R I V E
G E I S H A   K E R N E L
H E E H A W   S H O T
  E M M Y   E R E C T
S E R S   I O T A   N O W
W V A   B L U R T   D W I
A I D   A L V A   D O L T
B L I M P   E G G O
  C U T S   E L U D E S
B R A Z I L   D E B A T E
A B L A Z E   Y E L L A T
R I S K E D   E E L S
```

PUZZLE 54

```
S E E D   S A I D
P I X A R   I M P O R T S
L E T B E   R A P T U R E
I I I   S C A R   A M A N
T O N   H O S T   M U D
  G O A D   S L A M S
J U M P Y   O U I J A
B E I G E   T R I O
L T S   A S I N   R M S
O H H O   N A S A   E A T
O R I G I N S   M A T Z O
M O N R O E S   E N T E R
  G E N X   D E S K
```

PUZZLE 55

```
  M B A S     S L O B  
S E R U M   S H O V E L  
L E O N S   T I T A N I C
I S I T   B R R   L E A H
D E L I   E E K S   F B I
    E A R P   K R I L L
O B J E C T   R I O T E D
L L A M A   L E S T    
D U I   D R A B   A R F S
E R A S   A T A   T I L E
R A L E I G H   P I N U P
  Y A N K E E   R O G E T
    I D E S     E N O S  
```

PUZZLE 56

```
I T C H Y   D Y L A N  
C H L O E   R O A M E D
A R I E S   A U S T E R E
N O N   P I N T   D U G
  W E B B I N G   B L D G
    L E T S   D I E G O
A C R O S S   W A R D E N
B O A T S   F O N D    
A N T S   F O R E S T S
S G T   B I L K   B O P
E A R M A R K   A B O D E
  S A B L E S   G E N O A
  P A D D Y   T E E M S
```

PUZZLE 57

```
M E D I C   A C C T S
F I G A R O   S H E E P
E D G I E R   P A L L O R
T A O S   N E E D   A K A
A S S   S C A N   E V A N
    S L O G   T Y I N G
  M A K E B E L I E V E
L I V I D   R I N D    
A N O N   E L M S   V P S
M I C   M A Y I   C I A O
A B A T E S   T O A S T S
  A D I M E   E N R I C O
  R O P E R   D A R T H
```

PUZZLE 58

```
  O R N O T   B A H S  
  C R O S B Y   C L A W S
B A L D F A C E D L I E S
A G E S   M O L E   R E T
R N A   B A B E   T S P S
T E N S E   B N A I    
S Y S T E M   A R M A D A
    U T A H   L E V E E
S P A N   F I D O   E L S
E O N   G I N A   O N T O
G E N E R A T I O N G A P
A M U S E   A L I C E S
  S L E W   T Y L E R  
```

PUZZLE 59

```
  G A G   U P C S  
S H A R I   A T T A C K S
C A L M S   D U S T R A G
O N L Y   T A R   C E N T
R O O   H Y M N   H A G S
N I P P E R S   L I M A
    A D O   B I N    
  B U S Y   L E N G T H S
S O S A   M A L E   O A T
T O E D   A P T   R A V I
E N D E A R S   R A M E N
R E U N I T E   S T A N K
  P A L S   T E N  
```

PUZZLE 60

```
  S T A F F   U R A N U S
T E R R O R   S E V E R E
S C A M P I   E N G A G E
A L P   S I D E S T E P
R U D D   K A T    
  D O E S   M O S A I C
  E O N S   E D N A
  D R Y E R S   R A H S
    E K G   M A U I
B O O K F A I R   L A T
O R C H I D   A N V I L S
B E H A V E   T H I N L Y
S O O N E R   E L E G Y
```

PUZZLE 61

S	M	U	D	G	E				A	C	H	E	D
M	E	N	O	R	A	H			F	L	A	I	R
E	T	A	G	E	R	E			L	I	N	D	A
L	E	N		G	N	A	W		I	G	E	T	
T	O	T	S		S	T	E	T		I	R	S	
	R	I	P	E			B	R	A	N			
	S	C	A	L	P		B	E	R	G	S		
	I	S	L	E			Y	E	A	H			
A	M	P		S	A	C	K		S	R	A	S	
L	O	A	N		L	I	E	S		O	W	E	
F	U	T	O	N		N	E	P	T	U	N	E	
I	R	E	N	E		C	L	E	A	N	E	D	
E	N	D	O	W		S	W	E	D	E	S		

PUZZLE 62

	K	E	G	S			S	H	I	V		
A	N	G	R	Y		L	A	U	R	E	L	
H	A	G	A	R		E	X	P	I	R	E	D
A	V	O	N		A	T	O		S	T	A	R
B	E	N	D		N	I	N	E		I	D	O
		P	E	N	N		R	O	G	E	N	
S	E	S	A	M	E		I	G	N	O	R	E
H	E	I	S	T		F	O	O	L			
A	R	C		S	K	E	W		O	C	T	S
L	I	K	E		I	N	A		O	H	I	O
L	E	B	L	A	N	C		S	K	I	M	P
	R	E	S	I	D	E		S	E	L	E	S
	D	A	M	S			A	R	I	D		

PUZZLE 63

	A	B	A	T		E	M	E	R	I	L	
B	E	I	G	E		V	E	R	O	N	A	
A	S	N	E	A	T	A	S	A	P	I	N	
J	O	G		S	O	D	A		E	T	C	H
A	P	O		H	O	E	S		I	O	U	
		S	O	N	S		M	A	M	E		
U	N	C	A	P		O	G	L	E	S		
H	O	H	O		A	S	P	S				
U	S	A		A	L	I	T		A	H	A	
H	I	R	T		S	A	R	I		D	E	L
	E	L	E	C	T	R	I	C	B	I	L	L
	S	E	L	D	O	M		A	R	O	M	A
	T	Y	L	E	R	S		L	A	S	S	

PUZZLE 64

D	A	T	E	S		A	N	N	U	A	L
I	L	O	V	E		R	A	I	N	H	A	T
S	P	O	I	L		I	M	P	L	O	R	E
C	O	L	L	A	P	S	E		E	T	A	L
			H	E	D	D	A					
S	H	I	E	L	D		A	D	O	P	T	
C	I	T	R	U	S		A	N	E	M	I	A
I	D	E	A	L		B	A	D	G	E	R	
			S	U	P	E	R					
T	A	T	A		O	V	A	T	I	O	N	S
A	I	R	B	A	S	E		E	T	H	E	L
S	M	A	L	L	E	R		R	O	M	E	O
	S	P	E	E	D	Y		I	N	E	R	T

PUZZLE 65

	M	A	I	D		U	S	E	D	
F	A	L	S	E		S	H	O	U	T	E	D
A	D	I	M	E		H	A	N	S	O	L	O
D	E	B		P	I	E	R		K	I	D	D
	A	I	R	S	T	R	I	P		L	E	G
		E	L	I	S		O	B	E	S	E	
A	N	G	L	E	S		F	L	I	R	T	S
L	E	A	S	E		V	O	I	D			
C	A	L		P	R	I	N	C	E	S	S	
A	T	O	P		O	O	Z	E		P	C	S
P	E	R	U	S	A	L		C	L	O	A	K
P	R	E	P	A	R	E		A	G	O	N	Y
		S	Y	S	T		R	E	N	T		

PUZZLE 66

	M	A	Y	O			G	R	A	B	S	
A	B	A	L	O	N	E		R	E	L	I	C
D	O	N	T	M	I	N	D	I	F	I	D	O
E	N	D	S		C	A	R	D		F	E	W
E	N	E		D	E	C	O		P	E	N	S
R	I	L	E	Y		T	I	R	E			
	E	A	T	E	R		D	U	L	L	S	
	T	R	A	M		T	E	A	C	H		
R	I	P	A		N	O	A	H		P	R	O
I	N	A		E	G	O	S		I	D	A	S
G	L	I	M	M	E	R	O	F	H	O	P	E
H	A	N	O	I		E	N	R	A	G	E	S
T	W	E	E	T			G	O	D	S		

PUZZLE 67

```
  F L A G     A C T O R
S C R O L L S   S H I N Y
C H A P E A U   K O R E A
A I M   E Z R A   P A W N
T R E K   E F G H   D A S
  P R I G   A U D R E Y
    M A G N A T E
  B O S S E D   V E R A
F A R   P A T S   K E E P
R A S H   R U T S   M T V
O B O E S   R E P A I N T
N A N A S   F I E S T A S
T A S T E   N C I S
```

PUZZLE 68

```
  P E T C A T     C A B S
M A N H O L E   J C R E W
O N T O P O F   U L T R A
A C E   S O L O S   S L Y
T A R S   F O R T   Y E S
S K E I N   N A N A
  E D D I E   L O V E D
    E A R N   W I L E S
O K S   G R I P   V A S E
C O L   A S C O T   S S N
T H E I R   K N O T T E D
E L E N A   E C L A I R S
T S K S   D E D U C T
```

PUZZLE 69

```
S P I C E   S A L T
N A N A S   L I B E R A L
A L L I S   E L U S I V E
I M I N   A G O G   P E T
L E N   M U S S   B O R G
  R E C O R D   H A D T O
  P R A I R I E
W O M A N   A S T R O S
A H A S   A M T S   N C O
C A R   A L O U   T H O U
K R I S T I N   H Y A T T
Y E A R N E D   E R N I E
  S O O N   R A D A R
```

PUZZLE 70

```
    C O U P E   S P E D
  K A N S A S   B E L L E
F A S T E N S   A N A M E
I R S   R E A C T   T E D
L E I S   L Y F T   O R S
M E D I C   S O I L
  M Y B A D   S N E E R
    S L I T   G A V E L
S I S   Y V E S   N A P A
I D A   P E T C O   D O I
N O T E S   L O U D E S T
A L A M O   E N T I R E
I S N T   Y E S E S
```

PUZZLE 71

```
  S A B L E   A B I R D
I N D I A N   R I P E R
S O U T H C H I N A S E A
S O L   R H E A   D E A N
O P T S   A L S O   R M N
  R A N D   P A V E S
  S L A N T   R A W E R
G U E S T   Y E L L
I N C   S L O P   S T A G
S R T A   O K R A   R I O
T O U C H F O O T B A L L
  O R N O T   V O I C E D
  F E E D S   E N D E D
```

PUZZLE 72

```
  M G T     L E G I T
S A L A D S   A V E N U E
O M E L E T   K A R A T S
P I N E T R E E S   H O P
H E S   A O K S   L O R N
    M I N G   F I L E
T W A N G   C A P E D
E E L S   H O R S
O N I T   M A N E   S P A
W A R   B A N D A N N A S
E N D E A R   O S C A R S
S T E A M Y   S T O P I T
  S R T A S     S S S
```

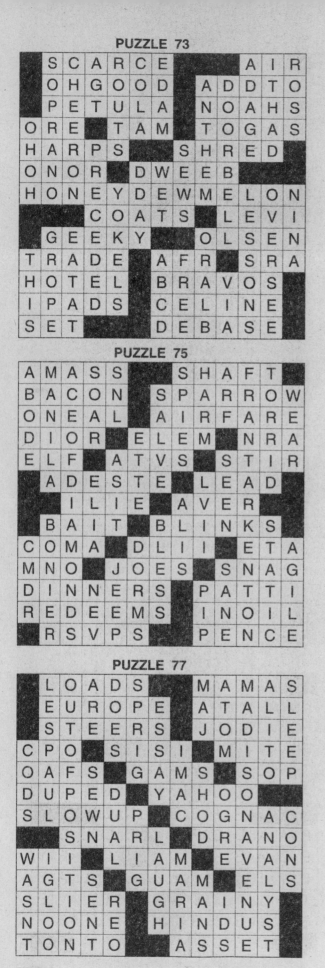

PUZZLE 73

S	C	A	R	C	E				A	I	R
O	H	G	O	O	D		A	D	D	T	O
P	E	T	U	L	A		N	O	A	H	S
O	R	E		T	A	M		T	O	G	A	S
H	A	R	P	S			S	H	R	E	D
O	N	O	R		D	W	E	E	B
H	O	N	E	Y	D	E	W	M	E	L	O	N
		C	O	A	T	S		L	E	V	I
	G	E	E	K	Y		O	L	S	E	N
T	R	A	D	E		A	F	R		S	R	A
H	O	T	E	L		B	R	A	V	O	S
I	P	A	D	S		C	E	L	I	N	E
S	E	T			D	E	B	A	S	E

PUZZLE 74

K	O	P	S		A	C	C	T	S
T	R	E	A	S	O	N		T	I	A	R	A
H	A	Y	R	I	D	E		T	O	P	O	F
I	N	N	S		A	S	I	A		T	O	E
G	T	O		A	S	S	N		R	A	P	S
H	E	T	U	P		K	W	A	I
	R	E	S	E	T		S	I	G	N	S
	S	E	X	Y		G	U	S	T	O
I	M	P	S		P	A	M	S		C	U	B
N	E	E		Y	O	G	I		O	H	N	O
A	R	E	N	A		E	M	A	N	A	T	E
N	I	C	E	R		D	I	S	M	I	S	S
E	T	H	A	N		C	H	E	R

PUZZLE 75

A	M	A	S	S		S	H	A	F	T
B	A	C	O	N		S	P	A	R	R	O	W
O	N	E	A	L		A	I	R	F	A	R	E
D	I	O	R		E	L	E	M		N	R	A
E	L	F		A	T	V	S		S	T	I	R
	A	D	E	S	T	E		L	E	A	D
		I	L	I	E		A	V	E	R
	B	A	I	T		B	L	I	N	K	S
C	O	M	A		D	L	I	I		E	T	A
M	N	O		J	O	E	S		S	N	A	G
D	I	N	N	E	R	S		P	A	T	T	I
R	E	D	E	E	M	S		I	N	O	I	L
R	S	V	P	S		P	E	N	C	E

PUZZLE 76

L	A	M	E	R		L	A	D	L	E
I	C	I	E	R		S	U	N	D	I	A	L
S	U	L	K	S		P	R	O	T	E	G	E
A	R	K	S		S	E	E	N		C	L	I
S	A	C		A	L	A	S		R	H	E	A
	S	H	I	V	E	R		P	I	T	T
		O	W	E	D		L	I	C	E
	R	C	A	S		D	U	P	O	N	T
L	E	O	S		G	I	G	S		S	H	E
A	L	L		D	E	E	S		R	T	E	S
R	E	A	P	I	N	G		R	E	E	L	S
A	N	T	O	N	I	O		A	N	I	M	E
	T	E	P	E	E		E	D	N	A	S

PUZZLE 77

L	O	A	D	S		M	A	M	A	S
E	U	R	O	P	E		A	T	A	L	L
S	T	E	E	R	S		J	O	D	I	E
C	P	O		S	I	S	I		M	I	T	E
O	A	F	S		G	A	M	S		S	O	P
D	U	P	E	D		Y	A	H	O	O
S	L	O	W	U	P		C	O	G	N	A	C
	S	N	A	R	L		D	R	A	N	O
W	I	I		L	I	A	M		E	V	A	N
A	G	T	S		G	U	A	M		E	L	S
S	L	I	E	R		G	R	A	I	N	Y
N	O	O	N	E		H	I	N	D	U	S
T	O	N	T	O		A	S	S	E	T

PUZZLE 78

G	O	A	T		N	C	I	S
A	C	R	E		B	O	O	M		A	Y	E
S	T	A	N		A	N	T	I		L	O	X
C	A	R	O	M		C	A	T	S	E	Y	E
A	V	A	R	I	C	E		H	A	V	O	C
N	E	T		M	I	R	E		M	E	S	S
			B	E	A	T	L	E	S
A	M	F	M		O	M	A	R		P	E	W
M	E	O	W	S		A	L	A	B	A	M	A
B	L	U	S	H	E	S		S	L	Y	E	R
L	O	L		O	U	T	S		A	P	R	S
E	N	S		O	R	E	O		S	A	G	A
	T	O	R	N		S	L	E	W

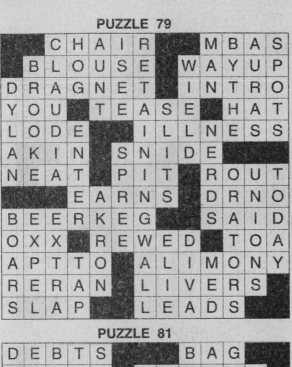

PUZZLE 79

```
C H A I R . M B A S
B L O U S E . W A Y U P
D R A G N E T . I N T R O
Y O U . T E A S E . H A T
L O D E . I L L N E S S
A K I N . S N I D E
N E A T . P I T . R O U T
. . E A R N S . D R N O
B E E R K E G . S A I D
O X X . R E W E D . T O A
A P T T O . A L I M O N Y
R E R A N . L I V E R S
S L A P . L E A D S
```

PUZZLE 80

```
. . I O W A . O B A M A
B A G G I E S . R O D I N
E N R O L L S . G O I N G
S T A T . S U B . K E E L
S I B . O H M E . C U R E
. C A P N . E R M A
. S T O C K . N O S I R
. L E I S . M E R E
L E V I . D A B S . I L L
A M I S . D I R . A S I A
M A C H O . D E C R E E D
B I K E D . S A T I S F Y
S L I D E . O K R A
```

PUZZLE 81

```
D E B T S . B A G
I Q U I T . W H Y N O T
G U L P S . H E R D E R S
S A G . B I N D . S E A
. L E N T I L S . B O A S
. . A I D E . L A U D S
C H I V E S . C U R T S Y
H A N E S . B O R G
O V A L . H A W K E Y E
P A R . A O K S . E A R
S N A P P L E . S A L S A
. A G R E E D . I D L E R
. E E R . P O S S E
```

PUZZLE 82

```
E R G O . R I C K S
P I N U P . A C T I N G
S T A I R . W O R N O U T
O A T . O P E N S . R I N
M S S . B O G S . P E L T
. . S L O G . F O R T
. A F T E R . B E T S Y
. F R O M . D A D S
C R E W . M I K E . T B A
P A S . S A V E R . R I G
R I H A N N A . A M I L E
. D E S I G N . L I M B O
. N A P E S . A S O F
```

PUZZLE 83

```
. G H I . P A C T
P R A M S . A U T H O R S
R A Z O R . C R O O N E R
I D E S . T A G . P S S T
N I B . M O R E . P I T A
T O O L A T E . O I L S
. . E G O . D R E
. S A T S . L I B R A R Y
S H I M . F I R S . R I M
T A M E . I N K . B M O C
E P I S T L E . Q U O T A
R E N E W E D . T R U S S
. G E A R . S T R
```

PUZZLE 84

```
. C A G E . R O T
S C U R R Y . A T L A S T
E A S I E R . R E D U C E
R N A . G E R M . T O N
T E C H . H A M M E T T
A S K E D . U N E A R T H
. . R I B B I N G
P A N D O R A . D O U G H
E D A S N E R . O P R Y
L V I . A B U G . L A P
T I L T E D . M O T I V E
S L E E T S . P R E F E R
. D E C . S E A T
```

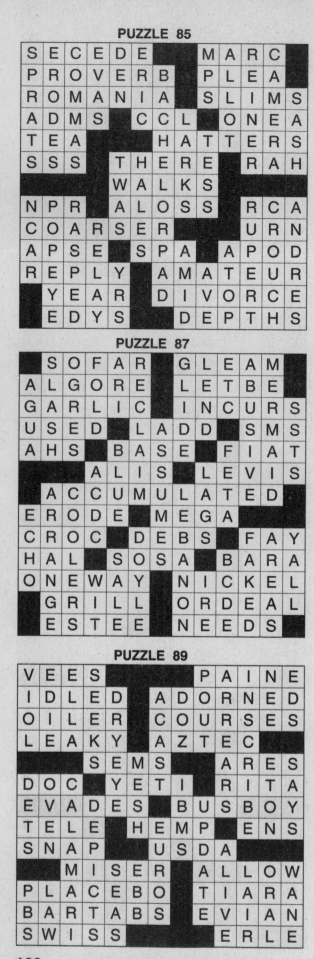

PUZZLE 85

S	E	C	E	D	E			M	A	R	C	
P	R	O	V	E	R	B		P	L	E	A	
R	O	M	A	N	I	A		S	L	I	M	S
A	D	M	S		C	C	L		O	N	E	A
T	E	A				H	A	T	T	E	R	S
S	S	S		T	H	E	R	E		R	A	H
			W	A	L	K	S					
N	P	R		A	L	O	S	S		R	C	A
C	O	A	R	S	E	R			U	R	N	
A	P	S	E		S	P	A		A	P	O	D
R	E	P	L	Y		A	M	A	T	E	U	R
	Y	E	A	R		D	I	V	O	R	C	E
	E	D	Y	S		D	E	P	T	H	S	

PUZZLE 86

	T	I	L	E	D		L	A	T	E	S	T
S	I	N	G	L	E		O	R	A	T	O	R
Y	E	S	S	I	R		V	E	L	C	R	O
N	C	O		B	L	E	A	C	H	E	D	
E	L	M	S		Y	E	R					
	A	N	E	W		E	S	C	O	R	T	
	S	I	T	E				A	M	E	R	
	P	A	S	S	E	R		W	I	F	I	
			M	E	D		T	A	C	T		
T	A	I	L	P	I	P	E			S	K	I
A	D	D	O	I	L		C	A	R	T	E	R
G	A	L	L	E	Y		A	D	H	E	R	E
S	M	E	A	R	S		L	O	O	N	Y	

PUZZLE 87

	S	O	F	A	R		G	L	E	A	M	
A	L	G	O	R	E		L	E	T	B	E	
G	A	R	L	I	C		I	N	C	U	R	S
U	S	E	D		L	A	D	D		S	M	S
A	H	S		B	A	S	E		F	I	A	T
			A	L	I	S		L	E	V	I	S
	A	C	C	U	M	U	L	A	T	E	D	
E	R	O	D	E		M	E	G	A			
C	R	O	C		D	E	B	S		F	A	Y
H	A	L		S	O	S	A		B	A	R	A
O	N	E	W	A	Y		N	I	C	K	E	L
	G	R	I	L	L		O	R	D	E	A	L
	E	S	T	E	E		N	E	E	D	S	

PUZZLE 88

O	B	A	M	A	S			C	O	R	P	
B	E	G	O	N	I	A		T	H	E	O	
S	A	R	O	N	G	S		R	A	C	E	D
E	K	E	S		N	Y	U		R	A	T	E
S	E	E				O	P	H	E	L	I	A
S	R	S		A	M	U	S	E		L	C	D
			T	Y	L	E	R					
A	M	I		T	R	I	T	E		S	R	O
D	E	N	M	A	R	K				L	E	V
O	R	S	O		H	E	S		W	I	P	E
G	L	O	B	E		I	N	V	A	D	E	R
	I	L	I	E		T	A	I	L	E	N	D
	N	E	L	L		G	E	T	S	T	O	

PUZZLE 89

V	E	E	S			P	A	I	N	E	
I	D	L	E	D		A	D	O	R	N	E	D
O	I	L	E	R		C	O	U	R	S	E	S
L	E	A	K	Y		A	Z	T	E	C		
			S	E	M	S		A	R	E	S	
D	O	C		Y	E	T	I		R	I	T	A
E	V	A	D	E	S		B	U	S	B	O	Y
T	E	L	E		H	E	M	P		E	N	S
S	N	A	P			U	S	D	A			
		M	I	S	E	R		A	L	L	O	W
P	L	A	C	E	B	O		T	I	A	R	A
B	A	R	T	A	B	S		E	V	I	A	N
S	W	I	S	S				E	R	L	E	

PUZZLE 90

C	C	C		C	H	O	O		B	A	W	L
O	H	O		L	U	L	L		I	L	A	Y
R	E	M		U	N	D	E	R	L	I	N	E
R	E	F	R	E	S	H		H	E	A	D	S
A	R	I	E	S		A	L	Y	S	S	A	
L	I	E	V		S	T	E	M				
	O	R	S	O	N		T	E	A	R	Y	
			R	I	P	S		T	A	O	S	
	N	A	M	A	T	H		W	O	N	K	A
B	A	D	A	T		O	P	I	N	I	O	N
O	P	E	R	E	T	T	A	S		N	O	G
C	E	L	L		A	O	N	E		T	N	T
A	S	E	A		U	S	S	R		O	O	O

PUZZLE 91

```
T A C T I C . S O S O .
A B L E T O . T W A N G .
R A I D E R . E L U D E S
R T E . M A D E . L E E K
Y E N S . L I P S . C S I
. S T I R . S L A C K E N
. . N E A R E S T . .
O R E G A N O . K R I S .
N O R . D I B S . L O C H
U P O N . M E A L . D E E
S E D A K A . M A R I N A
. R E V E L . B O N N E T
. D E G S . A S S E S S
```

PUZZLE 92

```
. H O S P . T E A R S .
T I C T A C . E X P E L .
O T T A W A . N I T W I T
R U E R . M A T T . R M S
O P T . P A L S . W I M P
. . C A R L . M E T E S
. S E E Y O U L A T E R
I P A D S . R O Y S .
R I S E . D E M I . C P A
A N Y . W A D E . S H U N
S A W Y E R . I N P A R T
C A I R N . N I C O L E .
H Y P E S . L A S S .
```

PUZZLE 93

```
. H E A P . H U R T S
C R O W B A R . A F A R M
R E B E C C A . R O D E O
A P B S . E T T E . I N K
P O L . A S T I . J A D E
S T E E L . L E V E L S .
. . C O W E R E D .
. B I R T H S . S I G N S
M E N U . I N I T . L O L
E H S . C P A S . W I S E
S A U N A . K A T Y D I D
A V R I L . E A R N E R S
S E E P S . C A N S .
```

PUZZLE 94

```
A W E S . A F R . A L I
L I M E . A L D E R M A N
E S P N . C A R D O O R S
C H I A N T I . S P U R T
S E R T A S . T E E N Y .
. S E E P . R O A S T S
. . N A Y . .
S P E D U P . A R A B .
T E X A N . S P I N E T
M E R C I . C O P P O L A
O R I E N T A L . P R O M
W E L L T O D O . L A N E
N O S . Y E S . E K G S
```

PUZZLE 95

```
S O C I A L . O A H U .
T W I T T E R . F R A N .
A N G E L O U . T E M P O
R E A M . N N W . A M A N
E R R . . N E G L E C T
S S S . A B I D E . R K O
. . C O N G A . .
I T A . L A G E R . A R T
D I S T U R B . W O W
A L P O . D A B . A H M E
S L I P S . C O M B I N E
. E R I E . K N E E L E D
. R E C T . A L L E Y S
```

PUZZLE 96

```
A R T S . C D S .
L A R A . C H O O . I C E
I M A N . H E M P . N O B
B A C K F I R E . C E N S
I D E A L L Y . S A R G E
S A D . E L L I N G T O N
. . B E E . G E E .
G R E A T D A N E . I D S
L A M B S . B I Z A R R E
A R I A . A S T E R O I D
N E T . F L U E . O N E A
D R S . E A R S . M O S T
. D I D . A N T E
```

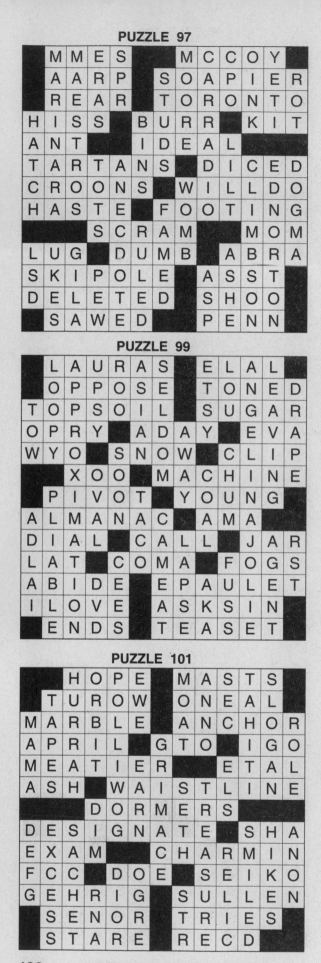

PUZZLE 97

M	M	E	S		M	C	C	O	Y	
A	A	R	P		S	O	A	P	I	E	R
R	E	A	R		T	O	R	O	N	T	O
H	I	S	S		B	U	R	R		K	I	T
A	N	T			I	D	E	A	L		
T	A	R	T	A	N	S		D	I	C	E	D
C	R	O	O	N	S		W	I	L	L	D	O
H	A	S	T	E		F	O	O	T	I	N	G
		S	C	R	A	M			M	O	M	
L	U	G		D	U	M	B		A	B	R	A
S	K	I	P	O	L	E		A	S	S	T	
D	E	L	E	T	E	D		S	H	O	O	
	S	A	W	E	D			P	E	N	N	

PUZZLE 98

			M	U	M	S		N	O	S	H
P	A	N		I	S	I	T		O	B	O	E
R	A	E		D	E	F	E	C	T	I	O	N
O	M	E	G	A		F	E	R	R	E	T	S
T	I	D	E	S		E	L	I	E		
E	L	S	A		D	Y	E			S	H	E
I	N	T	R	O				S	A	T	O	N
N	E	O		L	I	B		P	I	N	S	
			M	I	C	A		M	E	L	O	N
A	L	L	O	V	E	R		E	X	T	R	A
S	E	P	T	E	M	B	E	R		E	E	R
I	A	G	O		A	R	M	Y		D	D	E
A	F	A	R		N	A	T	L			

PUZZLE 99

	L	A	U	R	A	S		E	L	A	L
	O	P	P	O	S	E		T	O	N	E	D
T	O	P	S	O	I	L		S	U	G	A	R
O	P	R	Y		A	D	A	Y		E	V	A
W	Y	O		S	N	O	W		C	L	I	P
		X	O	O		M	A	C	H	I	N	E
	P	I	V	O	T		Y	O	U	N	G	
A	L	M	A	N	A	C		A	M	A		
D	I	A	L		C	A	L	L		J	A	R
L	A	T		C	O	M	A		F	O	G	S
A	B	I	D	E		E	P	A	U	L	E	T
I	L	O	V	E		A	S	K	S	I	N	
	E	N	D	S		T	E	A	S	E	T	

PUZZLE 100

L	O	A	F	S			L	O	O	T	
I	N	N	I	N	G		O	N	E	A	M
M	I	G	R	A	N	T	W	O	R	K	E	R
P	O	E		P	A	R	E	R		E	R	E
S	N	L		S	T	E	S		C	O	I	N
			H	U	S	K			P	U	N	T
J	U	L	E	P			A	L	T	O	S	
E	N	I	D		B	A	S	S			
A	R	T	Y		S	O	U	P		B	A	A
N	E	E		W	I	L	D	E		E	B	B
S	A	R	C	A	S	T	I	C	A	L	L	Y
	L	A	I	R	S			S	T	Y	L	E	S
	L	A	D	Y				S	E	A	R	S

PUZZLE 101

	H	O	P	E		M	A	S	T	S	
	T	U	R	O	W		O	N	E	A	L	
M	A	R	B	L	E		A	N	C	H	O	R
A	P	R	I	L		G	T	O		I	G	O
M	E	A	T	I	E	R		E	T	A	L	
A	S	H		W	A	I	S	T	L	I	N	E
			D	O	R	M	E	R	S		
D	E	S	I	G	N	A	T	E		S	H	A
E	X	A	M		C	H	A	R	M	I	N	
F	C	C		D	O	E		S	E	I	K	O
G	E	H	R	I	G		S	U	L	L	E	N
	S	E	N	O	R		T	R	I	E	S	
	S	T	A	R	E		R	E	C	D	

PUZZLE 102

A	R	M	E	D		E	P	I	C	S	
P	E	S	K	Y		V	E	R	A	N	D	A
L	U	N	G	E		I	C	E	B	E	R	G
U	S	B		S	A	C	K		S	E	E	N
S	E	C	S		I	T	S	Y		R	A	E
			A	N	N	S		O	W	E	R	S
	I	F	N	O	T		Q	U	E	R	Y	
A	M	I	G	O		H	E	R	B		
D	D	E		K	W	A	I		S	A	G	E
L	O	L	L		A	R	I	D		B	A	M
I	N	D	I	A	N	A		A	T	E	U	P
B	E	E	T	L	E	S		M	E	A	N	T
	R	E	E	D	S			P	A	T	T	Y

PUZZLE 103

R	A	S	P	Y		A	D	M	S	
U	P	P	E	R		T	R	E	E	T	O	P
G	R	I	P	S		R	A	G	D	O	L	L
S	O	R	T		J	I	F		A	L	D	A
	N	E	A	T	E	S	T		N	E	I	N
		L	E	E	K			D	E	E
S	H	A	K	E	R		A	C	C	O	S	T
T	E	N			T	H	E	A
O	R	G	S		D	R	O	O	P	E	D
M	O	L	T		W	A	Y		S	A	I	D
P	I	E	R	C	E	D		C	U	R	V	E
S	C	R	U	P	L	E		A	L	L	E	N
		T	A	T	S		M	E	S	S	Y

PUZZLE 104

	T	R	U	M	P	S		S	K	I	M	P
	R	E	S	O	L	E		I	N	D	I	A
G	I	V	E	S	U	P		N	O	I	S	Y
E	E	E		E	M	T		C	L	O	T	S
I	D	R	I	S		B	E	L	T	S
C	O	S	T		O	M	A	R
O	N	E	A	N	D	T	H	E	S	A	M	E
			I	O	N	S		E	L	I	A
	S	P	E	A	R		T	E	L	L	S
I	C	I	N	G		S	C	I		O	D	E
H	O	N	D	A		C	O	N	I	F	E	R
O	U	T	E	R		A	L	A	R	M	S
P	R	A	D	A		B	A	S	K	E	T

PUZZLE 105

C	H	A	F	E	S		R	A	M	B	O
B	A	C	A	L	L		A	U	D	I	O
S	T	R	I	K	E	I	T	R	I	C	H
	H	E	R		E	T	T	A
		Y	O	K	E	L		D	A	B	S
I	D	O	L	S		M	E	G	A	H	I	T
M	E	D	A	L		E	V	A	D	E
S	P	I	N	O	F	F		R	E	S	E	T
O	P	E	D		L	I	N	E	N
		B	O	N	A		P	A	R
I	N	D	I	A	N	A	J	O	N	E	S
V	A	U	L	T		C	O	R	N	E	T
S	T	I	E	S		P	E	T	A	L	S

PUZZLE 106

A	S	T	U	T	E		F	I	R	M
C	O	R	P	U	S		A	R	E	A	S
P	O	L	I	C	E	S		R	I	F	L	E
F	L	A	P	S			S	R	T	A
C	T	R	L		S	E	G	A		E	E	L
		E	M	A	I	L	S		S	S	E
D	I	S	T	I	N	G	U	I	S	H	E	D
I	N	T		A	T	H	E	N	A
A	S	A		S	A	T	S		B	R	E	W
N	U	N	S			G	R	O	V	E
E	L	D	E	R		S	C	R	I	B	E	S
S	T	E	E	R		R	E	I	N	I	N
	S	E	M	S		S	E	D	A	N	S

PUZZLE 107

	B	D	A	Y			I	S	M
	G	R	E	T	A		F	I	A	N	C	E
M	E	A	N	E	R		I	N	D	O	O	R
A	N	T	S		D	E	L	M	O	N	T	E
L	U	T	E	S		G	L	E	N
L	I	I		P	A	G	E		I	S	R
S	N	E	E	R	S		T	A	S	T	E	D
	E	R	R		C	U	S	S		A	P	O
		A	C	E	S		S	H	R	E	W
S	E	A	S	O	N	A	L		E	V	A	N
E	X	C	E	E	D		A	P	R	I	L	S
L	E	A	R	N	S		M	O	O	N	S
L	C	D			B	L	D	G

PUZZLE 108

T	U	S	K	S		S	E	W	N
A	S	H	E	S		P	R	I	N	C	E	S
H	A	R	P	S		L	I	N	E	A	G	E
O	B	I	T		N	I	C	K		N	Y	U
E	L	M		P	O	T	S		M	A	P	S
	E	P	C	O	T		F	O	R	T	S
		S	A	L	E		L	I	L	Y
D	O	C	K	S		O	B	E	Y	S
W	R	A	Y		T	O	G	S		E	A	T
A	D	M		G	O	T	O		A	L	I	E
R	E	P	A	I	N	T		B	U	L	G	E
F	R	I	S	B	E	E		C	R	O	O	N
	K	E	R	R		D	A	W	N	S

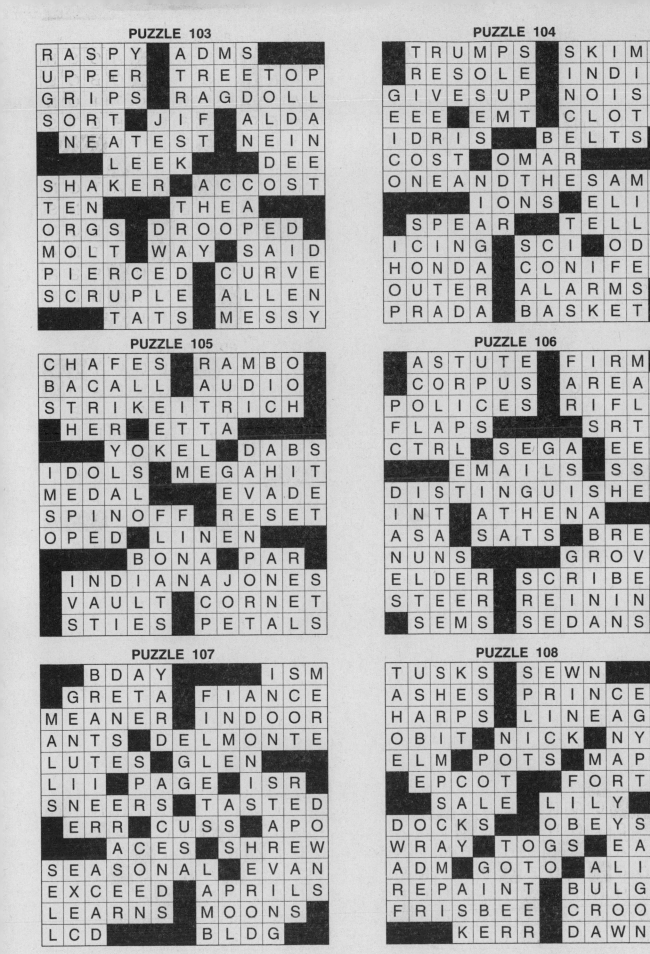